GATE BIENNALE

Cat and Mouse (Sheep)
Gregory Motton

Services
Elfriede Jelinek
Translation by Nick Grindell

First published in Great Britain 1996
by Methuen Drama
an imprint of Reed International Books Ltd
Michelin House, 81 Fulham Road, London SW3 6RB
and Auckland, Melbourne, Singapore and Toronto
in association with the Gate Theatre
11 Pembridge Road, London W11 3HQ

Cat and Mouse (Sheep) first published in 1995 by Flood Books
copyright © 1995 by Gregory Motton
Services translation copyright © 1996 by Nick Grindell
The authors and translator have asserted their moral rights

ISBN 0 413 70760 1

A CIP catalogue record for this book is available from the
British Library

Typeset by Wilmaset Ltd, Birkenhead, Wirral

Printed in Great Britain by Cox & Wyman Ltd, Reading

GATE BIENNALE
A CELEBRATION OF CONTEMPORARY EUROPEAN THEATRE AT THE GATE THEATRE

Gate Biennale is a unique celebration of contemporary European writing and writers. Based on a European model this is a British first, a biennial festival of the newest, freshest work from our continent. The Gate has spent considerable time researching the most exciting European playwrights and their plays from 1993 to 1995 and the season presents work from the United Kingdom, Austria, Sweden, Russia, Germany and Spain.

The emphasis of the festival is on the writers, all of whom we believe will come to dominate European theatrical culture over the next twenty years. Gate Biennale reveals the energy and wit shared by a generation with all six plays casting a scathing eye over contemporary Europe. The writers are political, scabrous and very funny.

We open with **Cat and Mouse (Sheep)** by **Gregory Motton** and **Services** by **Elfriede Jelinek.**

Gregory Motton, although adored abroad, is currently largely ignored in this country. **Cat and Mouse (Sheep)** is a satirical voyage through Britain. On its premiere at the Odéon Theatre, Paris, last year, it was described as 'a libertarian piece of theatre, destructive, plebeian, leaving no trace after its passage except the strong weeds of its sarcasm'. The Gate is proud to reintroduce this extraordinary dramatic voice to his own country.

Elfriede Jelinek is one of Austria's most acclaimed but controversial writers. Novelist, playwright and commentator, her work is cruelly comic in its exploration of modern existence. Her writing provokes extreme reactions: she is currently being vilified in a public poster campaign by the Austrian right-wing politician, Haider, but Frank Castorff's 1995 production of **Services** at the Volksbühne Theatre was the highlight of the Berlin Theatre Festival.

Gate Biennale will offer London a chance to see some varied and radical work as well as breathing life back into theatrical debate. The festival is designed to ask important questions about Britain's European identity, as well as if there is such a thing as a general European identity, at a time when the issue has never been more sensitive; but it is also a celebration, diverse and chaotic, of the most innovative contemporary work and writers in Europe today.

Acknowledgements

Gate Biennale was funded by:
The International Initiatives Fund of the Arts Council of England
The European Cultural Foundation, which promotes European cultural co-operation by running a grants programme, developing new projects and programmes in priority areas and serving as the centre of a network of fourteen independent institutes and centres for research and study
The Visiting Arts of Great Britain

Gate Biennale was made possible by the generous support of the following organisations and individuals: The Cultural Relations Department of the Foreign and Commonwealth Office, BBC World Service, Jenny Hall, The Jerwood Foundation, London Arts Board, Allied Domecq, and the Arthur Andersen Foundation, the Swedish Embassy and the Goethe Institute. Methuen Drama will publish all the plays in the season.

With thanks to:
David Pike, Bruce McAlpine, Ulla Krauss-Nussbaumer, Margaret Saville, Laura Hacker, Sue Higginson and Ian Oag; Martin at Nevada Bob's Golf Store for the golf clubs for **Services**.

The Gate

The Gate exists to introduce the work of international playwrights to a British audience. Its acclaimed seasons of work – including Women in World Theatre, The Spanish Golden Age, Six Plays for Europe, Agamemnon's Children and Storm and Stress – have led to a number of awards and widespread acclaim.

Now in its sixteenth year, the Gate has always aspired to produce the best of undiscovered world drama, providing a platform for the emerging talents of actors, designers, directors and translators. The permanent staff earn less than a living wage. All the actors, directors, designers and stage managers work for expenses only. The Gate survives because of their energy, commitment, talent and dedication to work. We constantly work towards achieving public funding. If you enjoy the Gate's work and would like to ensure its survival into the future, then please join our Friend's scheme.

Gate Theatre Awards

1990 LWT Plays on Stage Award for *Damned for Despair*
1990 Time Out Award for Consummate Classics Season
1991 Prudential Award for Theatre
1991 EC Platform Europe Award
1991 Peter Brook/Empty Space Award for the *Ingolstadt* Plays
1991 Time Out Award for the Directors of the *Ingolstadt* Plays
1991 Plays and Players Awards for Best Director and Best Production of *Damned for Despair*
1992 Time Out Award for Best Designer on *Damned for Despair*
1992 Olivier Award for Outstanding Achievement
1992 LWT Plays on Stage Award for *Bohemian Lights*
1993 International Theatre Institute Award for Excellence in International Theatre
1993 Time Out Award for Best Director/Designer of *Elisabeth II*
1994 Peter Brook/Empty Space Award for the Expansion of the Theatre
1994 Time Out Award for Best Designer on *The Great Highway*
1995 Empty Space/Peter Brook Award Special Mention

Karabe Award – Jenny Hall

The Karabe award is a unique one-year Associate Director bursary sponsored by Jenny Hall who is a long-time patron of the Gate, to provide a young, innovative director the opportunity of working closely with the Gate Theatre. The winner directs at least one full-scale production at the Gate and is involved in all aspects of the development and day to day running of the theatre.

1995 Indhu Rubasingham
1994 David Farr

Board of Directors

Mark Bayley
Kevin Cahill (Chairman)
Rupert Christiansen
Roderick Hall
Jonathan Hull
Lucy Parker
Lucy Stout

Friends of the Gate Scheme

Please take a form available at the box office.

Friends of the Gate £20+

- Your name is automatically added to our mailing list
- Priority ticket booking
- Two tickets for the price of one for the first week of all Gate productions
- Invitation to special events including the Annual Friends Lunch

Honoured Friend £150+

- All the benefits of being a Friend plus
- Listings in every programme for the year of subscription
- Reserved seating

Hero £500+

- All the benefits of being an Honoured Friend plus
- Annual thank you in a national newspaper
- Inclusion on the Heroes Board in the Gate foyer

Giving a donation

Donations of £250.00 and over are eligible for Giftaid; the scheme, operated by the Inland Revenue, enables the charity to increase the donation by a third of its value. Please call the Gate on 0171 229 5387 for more details.

Free Mailing list

To receive regular information about the Gate's unique seasons of international work, join our free mailing list – please fill in the form at the box office.

**Odéon Théâtre National de l'Europe, Paris,
Ducks and Geese and the Gate Theatre
present the British Premiere of**

Cat and Mouse (Sheep)

by Gregory Motton

cast

Old Woman, Man, Dickwits	Patrick Bridgman
Gengis	Rudi Davies
Aunty	Penelope Dimond
Uncle	Tony Rohr
Co-Directors	Ramin Gray and Gregory Motton
Designer	Nigel Prabhavalkar
Lighting Designer	Robert Longthorne
Sound Designer	Laurence Muspratt
Production Manager	Vian Curtis
Stage Manager	Charlotte Hall
Deputy Stage Manager	Jess Brown
Assistant Designer	Steve Dennis
Assistant Stage Manager	Tina Smith
Production Assistant	Jim Bishop

for the Biennale

Artistic Director	David Farr
Producer	Rose Garnett
Project Co-ordinator	Clare Goddard
Manager	Karen Hopkins
Literary Supervisor	Joy Lo Dico
Production Co-ordinator	Melissa Naylor
Press Officer	Rachel Stafford

Biographies

Patrick Bridgman (Old Woman, Man, Dickwits)
Theatre includes **The Tempest, Gawain and the Green Knight, Macbeth, As You Like It, Hound of the Baskervilles** (Midsommer Actors Company), **Don't Fool with Love** (Cheek by Jowl), **I, Bertolt Brecht** (Good Company), **The Revengers Tragedy** (Vox Theatre Company), **The Winter's Tale**.

Jess Brown (Deputy Stage Manager)
Training at Croydon College in Theatre Design and Lighting. Jess has stage managed for West 28th Street Production Company and has just finished a run of **Cinderella** in Suffolk.

Vian Curtis (Production Manager)
Resident Production Manager at the Gate. Trained at RADA. Theatre includes **Bloodknot, Don Juan Comes Back From the War** (Gate), **Heart and Sole** (Gilded Balloon/Newcastle Comedy Festival), **So You Think You're Funny!** (Gilded Balloon), **The Lottery Ticket** (BAC/Pleasance), carpenter for Hilton Productions and **Miss Julie** (New End Theatre, Hampstead).

Rudi Davies (Gengis)
Television: **Grange Hill**; theatre: Miranda in **The Tempest** (Old Vic); film: **Frankie Starlight**.

Steve Dennis (Assistant Designer)
Trained at Wimbledon School of Arts Theatre Course (July 1995). Television includes Rapido's **Girly Show**. Theatre includes Second Stride's **Baddenheim 1939**, Tenth Planet's **The Fox**. He is also the designer for Conundrum Dance Company and he is currently working on **Women Unbound** for the Lilian Baylis.

Penelope Dimond (Aunty)
Trained at Welsh College of Music and Drama. Theatre includes **Cat and Mouse (Sheep)** (Paris), **Macbeth, Wiseguy Scapino** (Theatre Clwyd), **Much Ado About Nothing, Hot Italian Nights, The Magic Storybook** (Oxford Stage Company), **A Flea in Her Ear** (Old Vic), **Slave Island** (Young Vic), **Alice in Wonderland** (Theatre de Complicite), **Ivan Vasilievich, Edwina a Cautionary Tale for Grown Ups** (BAC), **Hey Nicaragua, Doing Bush** (AK 47 Theatre Co-op). Radio includes **Molière** by Bulgakov (BBC World Service).

Ramin Gray (Co-Director)
Theatre includes **The Malcontent** by John Marston
(Latchmere), **Spring Awakening**, **A View from the Bridge**
(Liverpool Playhouse), British premiere of Denise Chalem's **At
Fifty She Discovered the Sea**, and world premieres of Gregory
Motton's **A Message for the Broken Hearted**, Liam Lloyd's
The Dark Side, Stephen Butchard's **Harry's Bag** and Andrew
Cullen's **Pig's Ear**.

Charlotte Hall (Stage Manager)
Trained at Aberystwyth University. Theatre includes publicity
team member for the National Student Theatre Company,
Edinburgh, Company Manager for the National Student Theatre
Company (Edinburgh '95), Production Manager for **Violent
Night** (Absinthe Theatre Company, Man in the Moon), Deputy
Stage Manager **Silverface** (Gate Theatre) and Stage Manager for
Dracula (Steam Industry at BAC).

Robert Longthorne (Lighting Designer)
Lit over 100 shows including world premieres of **Watching**,
Harry's Bag, and Gregory Motton's **A Message for the Broken
Hearted** and **Cat and Mouse (Sheep)** in Paris. Production
management for repertory theatre, tours and Welsh National
Opera including Peter Stein's **Falstaff**, and **La Sonnambula** in
France and Britain with his company Square 1. Lights, designs and
constructs sets for industrial presentations. Technical director for
Brouhaha's massive international outdoor **Invisible Cities-
River** project in Liverpool, September 1996.

Gregory Motton (Writer and Co-Director)
Work performed includes **Chicken** (Riverside Studios),
Ambulance (Royal Court), and **Downfall** (Royal Court)
published by Oberon Books, **Looking at You (Revived) Again**
(Leicester Haymarket), **A Message for the Broken Hearted**
(Liverpool Playhouse), **The Terrible Voice of Satan** (Royal
Court), **Cat and Mouse (Sheep)** (Odéon, Paris) all published by
Flood Books. Radio includes **The Jug** (BBC), **Lazy Brian** (BBC).
Other: translations from the Swedish: **A Ghost Sonata**, **The
Pelican**, **The Father** and **Miss Julie** which will soon tour Britain
in a production by Actors Touring Company.

Laurence Muspratt (Sound Designer)
Trained at University of London. Theatre: sound design for many
fringe productions including **Picnic** and **Guernica** at the Gate, **A
Walk on Lake Erie** and others at the Finborough. Work at

Liverpool Playhouse (and the BAC) on Motton's **Message for the Broken Hearted**. Recent work at Liverpool Playhouse on **Harry's Bag**. Laurence did the sound design for the premiere of **Cat and Mouse (Sheep)** at the Théâtre de l'Odéon in Paris. Laurence is still working on **Repeat The Word The Every 3 Seconds** which should end in 1996. Laurence is an RS6000/AIX specialist.

Nigel Prabhavalkar (Designer)
Trained at Central School of Art and Design. He was a finalist in the 1987 Linbury Prize for Theatre Design and for his design for Frameworks; **The Birds** represented the UK in the 1987 Prague Quadrennial for Theatre Design. Since 1983 Nigel has designed for theatre, opera and dance, as well a designing many sets for conference and music industries. Most recently: **Wicked Yaar** at the Royal National Theatre, **Night-Train** tour and Lyric Hammersmith and **Cat and Mouse (Sheep)** at the Théâtre de l'Odéon, Paris.

Tony Rohr (Uncle)
Trained at Actors Workshop. Theatre includes Max Starr in **Bohemian Lights** by Valle Inclán (Gate), Abe in **Looking at You (Revived) Again** by Gregory Motton (Bush and Leicester Haymarket), currently Juanette in **The Painter of Dishonour** by Caldéron de la Barca (Stratford-upon-Avon, then Newcastle and the Pit at the Barbican, May '96). Recent television includes **Casualty**, **Prime Suspect**, **Cracker** and **The Vet**. Recent films include **The Cat and The Moon**, **Runway One**, **Into the West** and **The Playboys**. Radio includes **Mary Stuart** and **Lady Chatterley's Lover**.

Tina Smith (Assistant Stage Manager)
Trained at Mid-Kent College, National Diploma in Performing Arts which included stage management, lighting, sound, set, costume, directing, arts admin. and make-up. Theatre includes numerous productions and one-off shows at the Central Theatre in Chatham doing lighting, sound and crewing; properties and sound fx at the Stag Theatre in Sevenoaks on **City of Angels** and follow-spot at the Rochester Arts Festival in July 1995.

Cat and Mouse (Sheep)

Gregory Motton

Characters

Gengis
Uncle
Aunty
Dickwits
Man
Old Woman

Cat and Mouse (Sheep) was first performed at Théâtre de l'Odéon, Paris, on 1 April 1995. The cast was as follows:

Gengis	Kevin McMonagle
Uncle	Tony Rohr
Aunty	Penelope Dimond
Dickwits	
Man	} Patrick Bridgman
Old Woman	

Directed by Gregory Motton and Ramin Gray
Designed by Nigel Prabhavalkar
Lighting by Robert Longthorne
Sound by Laurence Muspratt

Part I

A small greengrocers. A seventy-year-old **Woman** *comes into the shop.*

Old Woman   Three pounds of aubergines please

Gengis   Ah a dinner party I suppose?

Old Woman   That's right, a few meat-eating friends are coming round so we're having a big chicken salad

Gengis   Sounds super

Old Woman   Can I have a bottle of cherryade on tick?

Gengis   Certainly. Are you a bit short?

Old Woman   Yes my boyfriend has been made redundant again. That's the fifth time this year

Gengis   Do you want these? They're alright but they've gone a funny colour. I usually make a stew with them

Old Woman   Mmm thanks. How m–

Gengis   No have them

Old Woman   Oh thanks

She pays for the aubergines and then goes.

Gengis   I'm going to sell chickens in future

Uncle   But next-door sells chickens

Gengis   I can sell them cheaper

Uncle   He'll be annoyed

Gengis   He shouldn't charge so much, people round here can't afford it

Uncle   He's greedy

Gengis   He had that new floor put in for no reason, now he's got that loan to pay back

Uncle   He's got to walk on something I suppose

Gengis   What was he walking on before?

Uncle   That's a good point

Gengis   It's all his own fault

Uncle   So, the gentleman's agreement is going to come to an end is it?

Gengis   I've got to make a living too

Uncle   You'll be stocking milk next

Gengis   I will, and cheaper too

Uncle   He'll be very put out

Gengis   I can't help that any more

Uncle   It'll be war on this parade

Gengis   And another thing

Uncle   What's that nephew?

Gengis   I'm moving out of that flat of his upstairs

Uncle   Yes well it could be embarrassing, what with this price war and all

Gengis   I'm sick of paying the rent

Uncle   But where will you and Indira and the little horror live?

Gengis   We'll live in the back room here

Uncle   But it's only tiny. All of you in one small room. How cramped it will be!

Gengis   We'll get by

Uncle   But there's no window

Gengis   We're rarely in, we're always here working

Uncle   But there's no running water

Gengis   There's a tap in the yard

Uncle   There's no toilet

Gengis   We'll go in a bucket and I'll carry it out to the nearest convenience

Uncle What does Indira say?

Gengis She's very excited

Uncle Darrin

Gengis Yes uncle?

Uncle Where will your aunty and I stay?

Gengis You can sleep in there with us

Uncle What kind of bed is it?

Gengis A large single

Uncle So that's you, Indira, aunty, the baby and me all in one single?

Gengis A large single. I get up early anyway so you can all stretch out

Uncle Hardly stretch

Gengis Come and have a look

Uncle You've got the bed in already?

Gengis Yes, you'll be surprised how roomy it is

Uncle Alright

They go and look in the back room.

Pause.

They return.

Uncle Yes you're right. It's quite spacious after all

* * *

Uncle Well, how's it going with the old price war?

Gengis Things have changed a lot uncle

Uncle I see he's started stocking vegetables

Gengis I don't mind that. He still can't do 'em cheaper than me. And the quality of mine is better. I don't sell rubbish you know

Uncle   He sells those bags of potatoes

Gengis   They're rubbish they are. I've got all cold drinks in and jars of pickle and all the Indian stuff. It goes like a bomb

Uncle   You've changed too. You're ambitious, a man building an empire. Do you think you're still the considerate chap you used to be?

Gengis   I'm giving people good food cheap. I never rip anybody off

Uncle   But what if he goes out of business? Then they won't have a grocer around here, they'll lose out. You'll never be able to stock everything he does. Everyone will have to walk miles to Sainsbury's

Gengis   He won't go out of business, not if he watches himself

Uncle   Life is harder now. I don't sleep

Gengis   But we've got more money

Uncle   But I don't enjoy spending it any more. I feel sorrow. Your aunty, she's always been a swinger, she loves the high life but I'm more your man with a book beside the fire, a bit of an intellectual, studious, high-minded moral type, a rearguard man, a thinker, a political animal, a Fabian, a fundamentalist, I'm a justice fanatic a fan, I wear the right clothes, I'm left wing, I'm anti-Semitic I'm anti this I'm anti that I'm a star fucker and I'm interested in crystal balls and pot-pourri and Che Guevara and Mussolini and Winnie Mandela and co-operatives and things you stick on the fridge and notes and notelets and note-pads and living in London because there's a really thriving bisexual community there and lots going on and I own my own home and I run a little car because I care and I could really fuck you up if you get in my way brother sister mother black white racist sexist bloody bastards the whole lot of them, call me Ms don't fuck with my possessions ok because they're all approved and everything's kosher and I'm on the right side of the fence and I don't read much but I like a good book about suffering Chinese or suffering anybody anyplace because you know what I mean, there's so much suffering isn't there and I earn a bit of extra cash working for this charity organization that recycles shit and sends the best of it to the niggers and magically makes a massive profit and that's ok because they're helping people and I believe in that so I'm doing my bit and earning a fast buck at the same time, that's the future you know, recycled rags for the little babies with flies on their eyes. We're all going to be so fucking rich and so fucking pleased with ourselves my pussy is going to explode with pure satisfaction and that's all you can do isn't it because the world is going to rack and ruin. It's criminal, it's a crime, people have to be free, you know what I mean, they have to think for themselves, I always do. All I want is enough money to do exactly what I want because the state owes me a living course they do course they do course they fucking do. I pay my taxes, I'd willingly pay more, I was a bit of a punk rocker in my day, I went to all the gigs and I stapled my thumb, anyway they're all arms dealers and so would I be because deep inside I'm a poetical sort of a person, I'm a lyrical sort of a person, I'm a sensitive sort of a person, I'm a creative sort of a person and I know how to get some if you want some, but I've lost all interest in sex and I'm proud because I'm not going to be exploited and if I had any kids I'd put bromide in their tea because it's all about degradation and men bore me and so I just say 'look' you know what I mean and he said 'look baby, it's all just words, you're so afraid' and I said 'typical man, look at the way you're dominating this argument' and then like the poof he was he went and cut his own throat with a *Financial Times* letter knife. I hate weak men. So don't come to me, because I look after number one ok?ok?ok?ok?ok? So don't blubber just because you want to be mothered because it's not on offer so watch out because this is the cultural revolution and what's up is going to be down and what's down is going to be down even further, but all in name only because do you know what? Betting is immoral and those weaselly little Irishmen in the betting shops should be taken out and put to work digging holes in the road and made to do aikido. I'm doing a class in social awareness, Fuck you, you racist!

Gengis   So uncle, what you are saying is you want a bed of your own

Uncle   Yes

Gengis   Alright I'll see what I can do

*   *   *

Uncle   Your silken purse my darling is voluptuous to my fundament

Aunty   Our nephew. He's like a tub of cream cheese

Uncle   He's beautiful

Aunty   Life is beautiful Ned

Uncle   You're not uncomfortable with the new activities?

Aunty   He's getting very frenzied in his movements, do you think he's gone mad

Uncle   He's a man of the people if they did but know it

Aunty   I hate people, they're so unfair and horrible. Give me animals any day. A little doggie for example, all hair-cut and shampooed doing its little shitty in my hand, aaah the poor love!

Uncle   Shsh here's Gengis

Aunty   Gengis darling, you look so low

Gengis   Indira has left me

Aunty   Oh no! Did she take the kid as well?

Gengis   Yes

Aunty   Thank God. I hate their shitty little bottoms. Are you a broken man now?

Gengis   She said I'd made a big mistake, that she still loved me, that she'd never come back, that she hates a loser, hates a schmuck, hates a money grubber, hates me hates herself

hates the baby hates the flat hates the single bed hates shops
hates life

Uncle   You've upset her haven't you

Gengis   There's no going back now. I've nothing else to
live for. I must put up new shelving

Aunty   Darling

Gengis   Yes?

Aunty   Have you forgotten the charm of a quiet life?

Gengis   Yes, completely. All I want now is destruction and
victory and failure and death and victory and suffering and
defeat and death and victory

Aunty   Are we going to stay open later in the evenings?

Gengis   We'll never close we'll never open. This will be 100
per cent total shop, neither shop nor no shop

Uncle   There's greatness in those words, aunty

Aunty   There's greatness in the lips that speak them

Uncle   Greatness in the tongue and eyes that invent the
words and send them to the teeth that cut them. The temples
of his mind, the soles of his feet. He's ours now aunty, our own
boy

Gengis   I am king

Uncle   You are the Royal Emperor

Gengis   I am khan

Aunty   You are a cunt

Gengis   I will die a cunt. I will die, the world will laugh.
Blood will gurgle in that breath and she shall expire with me.

*   *   *

In the palace of the mighty khan.

Gengis   Uncle take me away from all this. I want to laugh and sing, I want to pull the legs off flies and burn them with a magnifying glass like the other children

Uncle   Here take my hand Barry. I want to tell you something. Look around you son, what do you see?

Gengis   Not much actually

Uncle   That's right my boy because do you know? There isn't much left. There used to be things, but as you know it's all been either broken or sold or sent somewhere else. There were things here boy that scum like you wouldn't recognize if it slapped you in the face. You hear what I'm telling you boy, you hear what I'm sayin'?

Gengis   Yes I do sir

Uncle   When I was your age this wasn't just paradise on earth this was the peak of fuckin' human achievement. We didn't just have buses, no sir we didn't just have flower fuckin' beds, though you bet your sweet life we had 'em, yes sir we had 'em. No we had something else. Shall I tell you what that something else was nephew child?

Gengis   Tell it sir

Uncle   We had philosophy! Yes! We had art. Yes! We had politics and history and sociology; we had MUSIC. I can hear it now callin' to me over th' airwaves. There was music in the streets and parks, there was music in the stores and booteeks, at the railroad stops and the city squares and in the gleaming white hospitals full of ailin' folk a' convalescin' you know what we had there? You guessed it boy – Ding dong, pling plong bing bong dow de dow dow. We had white-arsed muthafuckrs singin' the blues and blue-nosed Nigra fellas singin' their selves purple, we had Chinkies that were kinky with their rinky tink tinky and Puerto Ricans and Mohicans makin' sounds that were out of bounds. And if ya didn't like it you know what ya did boy?

Gengis   No sir

Uncle   Ya went and ya fucked yourself, yes sir that's what yer did 'cause there wasn't no way no place you could git away from it because The People Were Telling It Like It Was you know what I'm sayin'?

Gengis   I reckon I do unk

Uncle   Now listen me boy and listen me good. I ain't gonna continny this here con-ver-sation. I ain't gonna go on an' itemise all of them things we had back there in th' good old golden days cuz I might embarrass you. I ain't gonna say like as we had them librarees where folks come and pessued theys lernin and a-readin and a-lookin up thungs because there ain't no muthafuckr kin read no more in this nation

Gengis   Get to the point uncle darling

Uncle   The point is that what little remains of the great civilization that once held sway here I want you to think of as yours to dispose of how you will

Gengis   I shall do

Uncle   Good

Gengis   What's that great blue thing outside the window uncle?

Uncle   The sky

Gengis   Remarkable how it's changed. You see how it now seems to have a head and out of the top of its head, why look, it's raining!

Uncle   Is it? No, that's a whale

Gengis   Is it true they are why you can't get a council transfer even on medical grounds? Because they've given all the flats to the whales?

Uncle   Yes it is true

Gengis   What rotten luck for the plankton

Uncle   Listen carefully boy; The plankton are scum. Evil and lascivious. They know nothing, feel less. My plan is to infect the gorgeous belly of the spermy leviathan with their odious little bodies until they are all beached, the mucousy little white scum and the great blue monster of carnal desire together. Then we shall haul them to the knackers' yard and make them into glue for my model aeroplanes

Gengis   But aunty told me the whales cry most beautifully. Real tears. She has tapes

Uncle   All fakes. Merely an ingenious amplification of her bowel movements set to music

Gengis   She's a woman of many pretensions my aunt. Shall I have her liquidated?

Uncle   Not yet boy, she may want to buy something. Now before I forget I want you to strip to your underwear

Gengis   But uncle darling I told you I need time, sweet words, the odd bunch of flowers. I want to feel needed first

Uncle   Gentle boy, be at ease, this is a purely altruistic deed on both our parts. You see, this fax came in

Gengis   What is it? It's so beautiful!

Uncle   It's a photo of an earthquake in Turkeytown, 10,000 dead

Gengis   Hmm, if you hold it upside down they all seem to be languishing most charmingly on piles of jauntily arranged furniture and possessions. Where is Turkeytown, can we go there?

Uncle   Sorry son it's too far. It's a land without borders in heartiest Afrique

Gengis   What a golden land. Do you think they'd like to buy something?

Uncle   It's possible, but we must move swiftly. The quake was followed immediately by a terrible civil war

Gengis   Heavens! We must help them!

Uncle   Then a famine

Gengis   Lord have mercy!

Uncle   Then a surge of their national debt

Gengis   Christ have mercy!

Uncle   And a plunge in their credit profile

Gengis   Lord have mercy! What shall we do?

Uncle   Put your clothes in a brown bag and we'll mail them with a press release

Gengis   Marvellous idea. I get it; the first one free, the rest they pay for

Uncle   That's it

Gengis (*stripping*)   Hmm I feel good. I feel excellent. Now I'm bored. I'd like to go and exhibit myself

Uncle   A trip to the theatre. I'll book tickets at once (*Phone.*) Hello Wally? What's on? – Hmm 'loins' a challenging exposé of a decade's housing policy, a thought provoking musical

Gengis   I like it

Uncle   Or, a radical reworking of the bard's great tragedy 'Omelette – You can't make one without breaking eggs'

Gengis   I like it better

Uncle   Twenty-five tickets please, yes. We'll have a row to ourselves

Gengis   Goody, we can crawl along the seats to each other waggling our tongues like this (*Waggles his tongue.*)

Uncle   Excellent boy!

Gengis   All I want is my fingers around the greasy pole

Uncle   And then?

Gengis   Work it gently to see what I can get out of it like the other members of my parliament

Uncle   What if nothing is forthcoming?

Gengis   Then I shall take to the streets in protest

Uncle   It's almost unprecedented for a head of state to get involved in demonstrations

Gengis   I shall have the army with me of course

Uncle   It may just swing opinion your way. There is a lady to see you

Gengis   I must strip search her at once (*Pulls on rubber gloves and a WPC helmet.*)

Aunty   Gengis darling!

Gengis   Aunty it's you

Aunty   May I have a little word?

Gengis   Of course, what is it?

Aunty   Well you see, you know how I love art, you know how I've always had loads of friends who are very clever and one lovely girl called Janet-with-crabs?

Gengis   Yes, that well-known working girl

Aunty   Well we've made a little experiment with my doggie's doodoos

Gengis   Yes

Aunty   We've made a weally weally big pile of it and made it all dry in the sun

Gengis   That's lovely aunty

Aunty   And now it's as big as a house

Gengis   Wow

Aunty   And well, Janet-with-crabs and I thought the little people who live in the horrid smelly bit of town would like it on their little smelly park, because they love their doggies too and they also love their doggies' doodoos, I know they do because they spread it everywhere, even outside the food shops, they love their little doggies they do

Gengis   Yes

Aunty   And you know how Janet-with-crabs is such a friend of the people and all her work is done to help them because you know she is people too you know she told me and she used to talk like this eeow eeorw eeow (*A strong London drawl.*)

Gengis   Did she?

Aunty   Yes and now although she talks like us now she's still like that inside, she said so, even though of course she's not really because she likes all the things I like, we're like twins

Gengis   Yes.

Aunty   Well we took the big big pile of doggie doos and put it in their tiny tiny park and the nasty scum are so thick they said it was a nasty pile of doggie doos and take it away they said, take it away and they said Janet-with-crabs, Janet-with-crabs all the time over and over and I cwied!

Gengis   Well aunty, they are too stupid. Your pile of doggie doos is wasted on them

Aunty   That's what I said, I said to Janet-with-crabs lets bring it here to Gengis and put it in his front room or in his garden or in his little lovely pretty park in the lovely northern suburb of H . . . where he lives because he is king

Gengis   No fucking way! What do I want a pile of dog shit here for, I've got enough with that little crap machine you pull around on a lead leaving its disgusting mess everywhere. My Samarkand calf slippers are ruined. Now fuck off

Uncle   There is a rude man to see you oh great philosopher king

Gengis   Send him –

Uncle   O mighty wordsmith of the soul

Gengis   Send him –

Uncle   O illustrious moral engineer, jack-of-all-trades

Gengis   Send him my regards but I have a lunch appointment

Uncle   He is most importunate

Gengis   I am sorry for him

Uncle   He is the very picture of frailty

Gengis   Give him a –

Uncle   He's idle, he's poor, he has everything

Gengis   I'm running a fever, my clothes are sticking to me

Uncle   He is most spectacularly downtrodden

Gengis   He is a dreadful bore, send him away

Uncle   My lord he is green with envy

Gengis   Is he?

Uncle   Glowing like an emerald

Gengis   Poor man send him in

Uncle   This way dog and make it snappy

Man   Good afternoon O dainty one

Gengis   You have made a horrible smear on my lino, you are much to blame. Now quickly, you have a suit for us?

Man   The people have sent me to say this to you; we are all slaves –

Gengis   Stop right there. I will have no such ignoble word used inside these walls

Man   Then we are the vilest . . . servants . . . kicked like dogs –

Gengis   Have some self-respect man, don't affront my ears with such filth

Man   What shall I say?

Gengis   Don't say slaves or vile servants. Say you are journeymen. Stand upright, start again

Man   We are journeymen –

Gengis Wait. I think apprentice is better

Uncle Start again

Man My Lord, the people have sent me to say we are apprentices –

Gengis Stop again. I think apprentices has a bad odour. Doesn't it put you in mind of a horrible hierarchy of status. Let him say 'we are master craftsmen'

Uncle Say master craftsmen

Gengis Sorry, let him say guildsmen

Man My Lord we are guildsmen –

Gengis Good I am pleased

Man – and our children are starving, we are beaten daily and our old folk are thrown into the streets, our cripples are made laughing stocks and our idiots are molested in all manner of ways by everyone. We languish in degradation and confusion, we are less than brutes, less than savages, we are like the quickening flies on a dung heap

Gengis Don't say cripple, say Sedate

Man Sedate my liege Lord?

Gengis Yes, not lissom or agile perhaps, not acrobatic and frantic in the way of the younger healthier guildsmen, but still sedate

Man I –

Gengis For remember; I may be a spastic in my head but my body glistens from tip to prick

Uncle Un bon mot, mon petit!

Gengis Do I complain? Do I use ill-sounding words to slander my brothers? Do I use the words of a pink nose brown shorted blue shirt red neck dupe? No. I have put my house in order. I suggest that you do the same, before you prejudge, predetermine and interfere with your brothers and sisters. I think you understand me, we'll none of it

Man No My Lord

Gengis Now, was there anything else?

Man Yes, I wondered if Your Majesty required une fille à champagne?

Gengis A what?

Man Une cocotte au compot

Gengis Eh?

Man A tart My Lord, my daughter

Gengis Ah yes, send her in

Man At once O Mighty One

Goes.

Gengis Nice fella. A bit thick. And, if I'm not mistaken, a spic, a greaseball, a wop and a dago. Stank the place out. Time for the royal bath

*   *   *

Gengis Aunty and uncle . . . Why?

Aunty Because we love you

Gengis I do want a companion

Uncle A girlie?

Gengis Yes

Aunty What about the prime minister?

Gengis Too early a riser to satisfy me

Aunty (*thrilling at his words*) We're winning, we're winning, we're winning the battle against loneliness. Can you lend me the price of a cuppa?

Gengis Wait, where are my ambassadors?

Uncle They're on their ways

Aunty They have jet lag and are sleeping it off

Uncle   How shall we amuse ourselves until their return?

Gengis   Perhaps I can meet the executioner?

Uncle   He's busy just now. Here, read this

Gengis   What is it? Hmmm, hmm, interesting

Uncle (*snatches it back*)   Give it back, not that, this

Gengis   Oh

Uncle   Go on, read

Gengis   I can't, it's all . . .

Uncle   Yes?

Gengis   It's

Uncle   Well?

Gengis   Maman told me never to

Aunty   Shall we dance, I've brought my spinning top, it whistles the fandango

Gengis   Doesn't it know any proper tunes?

Uncle   Like what? Like the pasa doble I suppose, like the old rhumbaba

Gengis   I know let's rape uncle

Aunty   Good boy, that's more like it. I must say, I was beginning to think you were a bit of a poof

They seize **Uncle** *and force her into the bending over position from there lifting up* **Uncle**'s *raincoat. The great khan goes about his business, but after a few moments he stops short.*

Gengis   Hmm this is not buggery as I knew it. Uncle is a woman

Aunty   That's right, but your little aunty is a man. Take me I'm yours

Gengis   You're not yours to give away like that. As regent I insist that you save yourself, have some modesty. This is a kingdom of losers, I want winners. The world will beg for our favours

Uncle (*adjusting his vest*)   We must be patient

Gengis   We'll enchant them. Death to the collaborators. Death to the traitors. Death to everyone!

Aunty   Darling

Gengis   Yes?

Aunty   There are rumours of a plot against you

Gengis   What boldness. Who would be so cruel?

Aunty & Uncle   It's definitely no one WE know

Gengis   What happens if they succeed?

Aunty ⎞   All that has been gained will be lost
Uncle ⎰   All that has been lost will be gained

Gengis   How can we refuse?

Uncle   Politely at first

Gengis   And if they persist?

Uncle   Then we'll expose them to the people for the overdressed fascist goons they really are

Gengis   What if my people are attracted by their gaudy effects? You know what pigs they are, living in squalor and ignorance. What if they made demands on the royal purse?

Uncle   We shall be ironic with them

Gengis   Excellent! What if they are ironic back?

Uncle   Then we shall be sarcastic

Gengis   Good. And if they are sarcastic too?

Uncle   Then we shall become absurd

Gengis   But –

Uncle   Yes?

Gengis   What if they are absurd back?

Uncle   Then we shall be sexy

Gengis   Sexy? You mean kiss them?

Uncle Perhaps

Gengis On the lips? Is that what they call democracy?

Uncle Yes (*Crosses himself.*)

Gengis But they eat tinned fish, don't they? They smell like a cat's fart

Uncle We must try to be nimble. We must love them. As they love us

Gengis But uncle, they love me most don't they?

Uncle They idolise you

Gengis Then it's me they'll want to kiss, who knows, maybe more? You know what a kiss can lead to, you know what a vast population we have

Uncle Erm, alas no more

Gengis No?

Uncle No. There was a little accident. Most of them died

Gengis Oh. How many left?

Uncle Oh loads. Enough anyway to please Your Majesty

Aunty Oh definitely

Uncle But not enough to leave you ragged

Aunty . . . no, no not enough for that

Gengis Well, that's a relief. You know, aunty, uncle, I'm beginning to feel a great warmth welling up, an affection for myself that wasn't there before. I realise that I am the focus of people's hopes and dreams and that through me many destinies will rise or fall; if I block the roads and torch the harvest, millions will suffer

Uncle Several will certainly be very upset indeed

Gengis Alright, what's next?

Uncle Dickwits, the poet laureate is rustling his leaves outside Your Majesty

Gengis   At last some uplift after the drudgery of affairs of state. Drag him in

Dickwits *is thrown onto the stage.*

Dickwits   A poem Sire on the occasion of our nation's umpteenth birthday

Gengis   Good, fire away

Dickwits   I would like first to say a few words about the nature of poetry, the dialectic between culture and society, between society and the economy, the economy and its corollary, between the corollary and the anomaly, the anomaly and its astronomy, physiognomy and ignominy, ignominy and chim-chiminy, chim-chiminy and tyranny, tyranny and –

Gengis   Get on with it

Dickwits   Where to start, where to start indeed. We started I think appositely in a bus shelter in Hammersmith where we were able to encourage the twenty drivers and conductors –

Gengis   The poem man!

Dickwits
  Why do we suffer so
  I don't know

Gengis   Very neat. Is there more? It's a little flat

Dickwits   Oh it twists and it turns

Gengis   Twist away

Dickwits
  I think I know, said a boy
  Said a boy

Gengis   Mm

Dickwits   A change of pace there

Gengis   Is it likely to change again, I'm getting lost

Dickwits
    I think I know said a boy
    It's our master's fault

Gengis   What nonsense! I demand a rewrite

Dickwits   That's only the first draft. I have something else already going around in my head. It goes instead like this:
    I think I know said a boy
    It's somebody else's fault

Gengis   That's better. But it's dull

Dickwits   Dull? I think you will find that it makes people sit up straight when they hear it

Gengis   If I want someone to sit up straight I'll put a railing up their arse

Dickwits   Of course Your Majesty

Gengis   And not before

Dickwits   Quite

Gengis   Aunty, tell me if I'm wrong but the poetry in this nation is lard dripping from an old man's chin on a Sunday afternoon after his dinner

Aunty   Of course Your Majesty is correct

Gengis   It's dreary piss on a wall. It's the splatter of shit from a fat nurse's bum who eats but cannot digest. All over the toilet bowl, then she neatly wipes it away because she's embarrassed

Aunty   Your analysis is unfaltering

Gengis   But she can't reach all of it

Aunty   Yes!

Gengis   Then she glares at you when she meets you on the communal stairway as if you've done her an injury, just because your shoes are muddy

Uncle   I know the type

Gengis   And leaving clay on the hallway carpet that's no more than a piece of card to hide the boards

Aunty   Oh yes indeed!

Gengis   The boards that are probably stained with her liquid shit, and she hates you because you see it and she's Miss fucking prim and proper

Aunty   Holier than thou

Uncle   Nose in the air

Gengis   Smug and vicious, peeping from behind her curtain 'look at him, look at her' but she's worse than the whole blooming lot of them

Uncle   Squatting over her dinner plate on the floor to try to give it some flavour

Aunty   Some bloody hopes

Gengis   No bloody chance of that

Aunty   Bloody snob

Uncle   Miss Perfect

Gengis   The tightest bloody fanny in Finsbury Park

Pause. He muses.

Sad actually, and that's art in this bloody country

Uncle   You see how it upsets him. What are you going to do about it?

Dickwits   I shall . . . involve the community

Gengis   The what??? You nincompoop. I will not have the royal poet crawling to a selection of brewers belches. And another thing;

Tense expectation.

These bus drivers. Louts. And they don't give a tinker's casserole for your poetry. What they want is dancing, and dancing is what you shall provide. Aunty, supply the laureate with bells and let him get on with it

Uncle   Come on you, out of it

Gengis   How I enjoy a debate. I told him I think didn't I?

Aunty   You have single-handedly revolutionised the written word. Would you like us to −

Gengis   No, he may want to buy something

Uncle   There is a superfluity of bastards in the realm Sire

Gengis   And none more superfluous than Dickwits

Uncle   No My Lord, little babies growing up without that most ceremonious of blessings, a loving father

Gengis   Gads, we must find these loving fathers and reunite them

Uncle   They have buggered orf Sire

Gengis   And left the little babbies? Swines. Let them stay away I say, better off without them

Uncle   There is the little matter of the expense Sire, falling on the state

Gengis   Expense? Scandalous. Chop off their heads!

Uncle   The bastards My Lord?

Gengis   Bastards louts sluts, all just baggage

Uncle   Shouldn't we try to force the little families to stay together in their little hovels where they belong?

Gengis   That's it, Home Sweet Home, by God in my day we stuck it out, kitchen knives, fingers in plug sockets, suicide pills, ambulance, police whatever it took

Uncle   I shall tell them O great king

Gengis   Tell who?

Uncle   The congregation of 257 sluts with babies that is gathered by the royal drawbridge. They claim you are the father

Gengis   That's impossible. Tell them I am promised to
another. I'm sorry but I have a mortgage to think about.
And it wasn't me

Uncle   They each claim knowledge of a mole on your left
buttock

Gengis   There, proof! If I were the father I would hardly
have had my back to them, now would I?

Uncle   I shall tell them

Gengis   And lest they say I am neglectful of a man's duties
tell them I shall build a monument to our passions in the
shape of a great tower

Uncle   Marvellous idea. And what shall this edifice be
called?

Gengis   Borstal

*   *   *

Uncle   The refugees from Turkeytown have arrived Your
Reverence

Gengis   Ok, throw them on the heap

Uncle   At once. They told me to pass on their thanks in
advance for the jobs

Gengis   Ha ha ha

Uncle   And the nice homes

Gengis   He he he

Uncle   Which they say are in such short supply in the war-
torn desert they come from

Gengis   Uncle, I have noticed that the people from this
particular part of Turkeytown are unusually unattractive

Uncle   Yes Your Majesty

Gengis   Why is that?

Uncle This flank of Turkeytown is famous for its inbreeding

Gengis I see. You know what they need in my opinion, in order to make them beautiful like us?

Uncle Yes?

Gengis Immigration

Uncle I shall arrange it immediately. Shall I round up the scum from the tower blocks and send them? Then these fellows can have their homes

Gengis No, send the tarts who lounge around in the city hotels with their snotty children at government expense, it will save more money

Uncle And where will we put our exotic friends from the plains of Turkeytown with their multicoloured blankets and their handmade folk sandals?

Gengis We shall put them in the hotels

Uncle Brilliant

Gengis You see something tells me they will enjoy the fluorescent lighting in the bedrooms. The modernity of it will impress them. I can see it now, their children's dark little faces pressed up against the cheap double-glazing marvelling at the well-ordered business of our streets

Uncle Ah yes, that reminds me, a study has revealed they have no toys, the little loves

Aunty Aah what a shame!

Gengis Then send them my broken plastic launching rockets that aunty has trodden on. Give their imaginations something to dwell on

Uncle I think they're going to be very happy here. Wait till I get them to school, I have a brilliant plan

Gengis Oh yes, they will start off by singing Humpty Dumpty I hope, it's my favourite

Uncle   No, no, Sire, not that. You see they won't be able to speak English

Gengis   Then we shall get them to sing to us in Turkeytownese

Uncle   No, unfortunately they won't have mastered that either

Gengis   Surely that is the language their mummies speak to them

Uncle   No, no, Sire, they speak to them in English

Gengis   Oh, good.

Uncle   Not SO good

Gengis   Why?

Uncle   Because their mummies can't speak English

Gengis   Then these poor infants will have no language at all

Uncle   They will have two broken languages, the advantage being that they are unable to form thoughts in their heads, which makes them perfect material for our education system

Gengis   Aha! I see, we shall mould them right from the start. Imbue them with the culture of their new country

Uncle   Oh no, Sire, that would be horrid! Humpty Dumpty may be alright for you and me, and for any royal children God may grace you with (*Bows gracefully*.) but it is entirely unsuitable for this crew.

Gengis   Oh, why?

Uncle   It's English. They are foreign. It will make them feel inferior

Gengis   Naturally

Uncle   It's our worst fear

Gengis   What about God then? And Jesus, you know how he wants them for a sunbeam

Uncle God and Jesus are English I'm afraid. These foreigners wouldn't grasp it.

Gengis I suppose not

Uncle Best not to mention it

Gengis What shall we teach them then?

Uncle We shall teach them their own culture

Gengis But we don't know anything about it

Uncle Precisely, so we shall make a mishmash of foreign cultures and teach that. It will be entirely neutral, the kiddies won't notice a thing, it will wash over them leaving them . . . well, numb in a painless sort of a way

Gengis What about our own little sunbeams?

Uncle You mean the white trash from the estates? They will be relieved of the terrible burden of identity and be left just as confused as the little Turkeytowners. They'll all be in the same boat

Gengis Sounds like a recipe for harmony

Uncle I like to think so

*   *   *

Uncle and **Aunty** *pulling the khan in a troika.*

Gengis Who do you think loves the people most, you and aunty, or me?

Uncle We love them in different ways

Gengis Tell me about the way you love them uncle

Uncle I love them because I know them, I share their toils and their burdens

Gengis I love them because I don't know them and don't share their toils and their burdens

Uncle I love them because they have a wise nobility

Gengis I love them because they don't

Uncle   I love them because they are generous

Gengis   I love them because I am generous

Uncle   I love them because they are like abandoned children

Gengis   I love them because I have abandoned them

Uncle   I love them –

Gengis   And I abandoned them because they are so ugly

Uncle   I love them because through my love they will grow in body and mind and spirit

Gengis   I love them because they will always remain the pigs that they are

Uncle   I love them because one day they will be like me

Gengis   I love them in case one day I should become like them

Uncle   I love them and one day they will say to me 'guide us, show us the way towards the light of universal well-being'

Gengis   I love them and one day they will roll me in the gutter and I will look up at their contorted faces and say 'so this is how you repay my love, you dogs'

Uncle   I –

Gengis   How I've suffered for you, how vile and ridiculous I have made myself on your behalfs. Have I not suffered the opprobrium of making your vicious wretched voice my own. Have I not built glorious imperial towers out of your baseness so high and exalted you have no chance of seeing them, you squinting low-life barenosed scum? Have I not rubbed my hands in your smell and said to the assembled royal banquet 'smell this you toffee-nosed, half-arsed money-grubbing hypocrites'? Have I not as king stood on the table and lifted my skirts and shown myself to the most respected princes and queens out of utter contempt FOR THE WAITERS? Am I not a parvenu, johnnycomelately bacon-chewing tyrant all so that on this day, in this your gutter, in this cesspit of yours I could look up at your raised hobnail and say 'go on stamp you monsters, but you'd be just like me if you had the balls and the brains and the great love for you all that I have!'

Uncle And what would they respond?

Gengis They'd take my wallet, and let's be fair, it would be their right

Uncle Your generosity is truly regal

Gengis They'd have a right to my wallet because it would be empty, and an empty wallet belongs to everyman. And how do you love them aunty?

Aunty I cannot love them because they, sadly, are not worthy of my love, but I do fear them, I do admire them, I do . . . want them

Gengis And what do you want them for aunty?

Aunty I want them for so many things. There is a nice girlie brushes my hair and cuts my nails, and a big big man who mends my doggie when she falls over and a tiny tiny woman who clears my toilet when it blocks and they are all three so delicious I could eat them and where would I be without them . . . but they are not us are they, and we are not them because they beat their children and make their wives do the washing up and say all the wrong things whereas we are nice

Gengis Aunty has a point, our people are not nice, they are greedy and mean

Aunty They think only of money, they are racists, sexists and imperialists

Gengis Yes, where do they get it all from?

Pause for thought.

Uncle If there's one thing I can't stand it's intolerance

Aunty Don't say that word

Gengis Intolerance?

Aunty   I shall scream

Gengis   You're right aunty, we shall only permit
harmony. We shall say to them, live as equals, give what
little you have to your brother in need, and he shall be very
grateful however small the gift, just as he is grateful for the
little we give. If a man comes to you from afar speaking a
strange tongue and is in need for he is an eternal pilgrim to
our state for his own nation has for centuries been plundered
and pillaged, then give him your home, be it ever so small
and ramshackle and damp and cheaply built and horrible
and ugly, for this man is in need and cannot afford anything
better. For you will see in this that you have much in
common. And if another man comes to your slum and says
behold I am without a home, then give him your son's home
or your daughter's home be they ever so humble and
windswept and destitute of natural beauty except for the
cheer you have brought to it with what's left of your
contemptible dying out culture of cockles and mussels and
inferior brands. Give this I say to your brother and though it
may fall apart in his hands because it is not what he wants or
deserves it is nevertheless more than you deserve; and do it
not with sour words or fallen countenance, but with the
correct words and bright smiles, for be warned that if you do
not do it to the utmost, even though your joys are so depleted
that you have nothing left to give except that which you no
longer possess, if, I say, you do not do this, then it will be said
that you are evil and the enemy of mankind

Uncle   Quite right

Gengis   I know what I should say if one of these foreign-
tongued johnnies came to my door asking for my big house

Uncle   What is that O mighty regent?

Gengis   Piss off back to the slum you come from

Uncle   Of course

Gengis   And if he didn't and insisted on taking up
residence, I should move

Uncle   Quite right

Gengis   I can't live in an area full of people like that. I might be mugged or raped and you can't get real coffee

Uncle   It's all just a matter of taste. We don't like ghettos and slums

Aunty   Some do, some don't

Gengis   And quite apart from that, who'd want to live next door to a load of racist, sexist imperialists

All Three   Not us

Part II

Uncle   Your Majesty I have been watching the progress of the royal policy

Gengis   Which one?

Uncle   That of equity for all, fairness, lies, deceit, the abolition of words and a lot of money for Your Majesty

Gengis   Yes

Uncle   And I have observed its absolute success

Gengis   Are my people happy?

Uncle   There is a rosy glow about them to be sure (*Aside.*) on their little bottoms

Gengis   Good. Then it is time for phase two

Uncle   What is that?

Gengis   A lock out, a block out, an eclipse of the sun and moon, drown their pets, bring me their women

Uncle   Most prudent

Gengis   Uncle

Uncle   Yes Matty

Gengis   Who are these people . . . My Subjects

Uncle   A most unworthy bunch. One of them is a dentist, several million do nothing at all. Another is a kind of . . . housing officer

Gengis   . . . Hmm that last one, bring her to me

Uncle   She cannot be moved. The whole economy would grind to a halt

Gengis   Then we shall go to her. Where does she live?

Uncle   In the house Your Majesty

Gengis   THE house. Is there but one?

Uncle   For the moment Sire. Building is underway

Gengis   But where do the rest of my people live?

Uncle   In YOUR house gracious Lord

Gengis   What if I want to sell?

Uncle   Eviction is a top priority. Eviction and cleanliness make a nation great

Gengis   Let them all appear before me then

Uncle   They are . . . a little shy

Gengis   Surely in a group they feel confident

Uncle   They are shy and . . . a little ill

Gengis   How ill?

Uncle   Some poor souls are limbless, some headless, some bodiless

Gengis   What bold disease has wrecked my population

Uncle   The disease of being too cocky by half, AND not knowing the answer to a few simple questions

Gengis   Is there no cure?

Uncle   We sent a team of . . . doctors in

Gengis   The result?

Uncle   We're still counting

Gengis Well are there any hands or feet that you could bring me I must remain on familiar terms with my people you know

Uncle I will have aunty bring a bag at once

Gengis Good. This state business has given me an appetite – please fart into my mouth

Uncle (*Does so.*)

*   *   *

Gengis Steady me aunty, the inspiration is upon me again; I shall grant freedoms never before dreamt of. I shall make everything illegal

Aunty The opposition Your Majesty . . .

Gengis Don't mention them. They have no poetry in their souls, no philosophy, their arguments are based on a dilated fundament, they sit down too long in the draught and now they blame me. Withdraw their prescriptions!

Aunty Quick Your Majesty, a decree!

Gengis Open the prisons!

Aunty Your Majesty?

Gengis Close the prisons

Aunty ?

Gengis Open them. Close them. Open them. Close them. Who can tell which is which

Uncle That is a paradox young master

Gengis No, it's a dilemma, but not for me. My words come and go with the wind

Aunty What a genius. His words have no meaning whatsoever

Gengis Oppress the Lowly! Liberate the unloved

Aunty Frightening scansion!

Gengis   What's bad is good, what's good is merely useful, green belt is red tape, red tape is blue riband . . . Aunty you are distant today, perhaps it is time once more for the royal bath

Sound of a bath being run.

Come on muckers who will join me?

They strip.

Uncle what is that legal document in your trousers?

Uncle   Oh it's nothing, merely wrapping for my member

Gengis   Please let me see it, take it out

Uncle   I couldn't

Gengis   I can see the writing on it from here. Whose names are they? Not your conquests surely

Uncle   O great king I can conceal it no longer. It is indeed, a testimony of loves bourne towards me, not conquests though but subjects

Gengis   My subjects?

Uncle   It is a petition

Gengis   It has a formidable length

Uncle   They say I should snatch the crown from your head, they say the abuses of your regime are . . . so many they have forgotten them

Gengis   All of them? Ungrateful wretches! What must a king do?

Uncle   . . . so I drew up a list of them myself

Gengis   Ah?

Uncle   They are as follows; you have usurped the role of tyrant which properly belongs to . . .

Gengis   Who's he?

Uncle   Nobody knows. You have spoken only the truth and forbidden fibbing in your cabinet

Gengis   True

Uncle   You have forbidden the use of paper. You have fed and clothed the hypocrite and abolished dishonesty

Gengis   Thank you. I was wondering if anyone had noticed that

Uncle   You have bragged of your weakness in a most ironical tone

Gengis   They cheered me for it too God bless 'em

Uncle   You have pissed on the beach

Gengis   It pissed on me

Uncle   Industry has suffered; 100 per cent employment, 1000 per cent productivity, Sales nil

Gengis   National pride if you'll pardon me uncle. The workers love me for it and I love them

Uncle   You have housed the homeless

Gengis   What statesman could do less

Uncle   In a giant slum

Gengis   In my own favourite city, in my own arrondisement, in my own house

Uncle   And charged them exorbitant rents

Gengis   (*Smiles to himself.*)

Uncle   And in a swingeing piece of legislative villainy that humiliated the rich and disenfranchised the poor –

Gengis   Ah the double-edged sword!

Uncle   – You taxed all mention of the underprivileged

Gengis   What a great burden was thereby lifted from the national vocabulary. A most revealing piece of statecraft

Uncle   So, with the opposition now withdrawn into self-imposed exile of silence in the capital's northern suburb of H . . . you empowered the bootless herd with the right of requisition creating unprecedented shifts of population and a reversal of political allegiances

Aunty   He is an evil genius

Uncle   You see Sire, they have sinned, you have sinned, we have sinned, I, . . . well I have corrected sin from my blackened soul and am now pure

Gengis   Forget that now, I have something important to say to my people. (*Goes to his balcony. Returns.*) I shall tell them; Lords, ladies and gentlemen, forgive yourselves, forgive your brothers and sisters, forgive me, try not . . . try . . . have faith. Don't you think that is rather moving?

Uncle   Yes it is moving. But I would like to move them in some other way (*He manipulates his rolled petition with barely-controlled ferocity.*)

Exit.

Gengis   Aunty, I am afraid. The kingdom once renowned for its modest charms has become a bunker where people perform deeds of darkness upon one another

Aunty   Oh it's only their way

Gengis   Their way of what?

Aunty   Their way of saying (*With great sentimentality.*) 'we are people too you know'

Gengis   Oh I see, and the murdering and torturing that goes on in our parks and woodlands for entertainment?

Aunty   Oh it's only their little way

Gengis   Their little way of what?

Aunty   Their little way of saying 'sometimes we're lonely, sometimes we're afraid, sometimes we don't really know what is wrong; so we take someone and we pull their teeth out with pliers, then set fire to them, a little group of chums together, girls and boys, supportive, caring, no nasty words'

Gengis   What does it all mean aunty?

Aunty (*ferocious*)   It means the devil is amongst us, put the boot in hard while you've still got the chance. Put bars up at your window, don't talk to yourself after eight pm, don't give an inch or they'll take a mile, string em up, cut them down. You see?

Gengis   Yes, I see

Aunty   It's just their little way of saying (*Baby talk.*) 'we're lost and lost and lost and lost and we don't know our way home.' (*More so.*) 'We want some more money'

Gengis   But wait. I want some more money

Aunty   Don't interrupt. It's their little way of saying 'we want free this free that and free the other'

Gengis   Bastards! Wait till I catch them

Aunty   They want you to be their scapegoat

Gengis   Do they?

Aunty   They want to blame you for the piss in their lifts

Gengis   But I'm a socialist. I would never piss in a lift

Aunty   Perhaps you haven't explained that well enough. You must communicate

Gengis   I'll make a play a book a poem

Aunty   That way they'll all understand. They love plays and books and poems

Gengis   But how? They're all so thick

Aunty   We'll put it on television and call it Bingo Wingo Zingo Zam Powee

Gengis   What if they come round to watch it on my TV set? I'm not having any of them in here, they all stink of air freshener. Do they wear toilet cleaner as perfume?

Aunty   Yes son they do

Gengis   Maybe it's too late to help them

Aunty   Aaah don't say that. Imagine their little faces looking up at you with their big eyes 'please help us don't to be such ignorant Tory Goons'

Gengis   The bigoted swines. The thought of them makes me want not just to piss in their lifts but to shit on their brains

Aunty   It's been done. They have done it to themselves. Out of sheer bloody-mindedness of course

Gengis   Ha! So British. So land of hope and glory. So UK

Aunty   Doesn't it make you proud to be not British

Gengis   Yes, urgh! I'm half Maltese

Aunty   I'm half Madagascan

Gengis   I'm half Chinese

Aunty   I'm half Indonesian

Gengis   I'm half Polynesian

Aunty   I'm half Melanesian

Gengis   I'm half MALVENIAN

Aunty   I'm supporting the African teams in the World Cup

Gengis   I'm supporting India in the alternative World Cup

Aunty   I'm supporting rabbits in the animal World Cup

Gengis   I'm supporting poor little pussies in the World Cup for animals with electrodes in their little brains

Aunty   I'm supporting animals that aren't in any teams because they are too sick because they've been eaten by doggies in the garden

Gengis   YOU HIPPOCRITE!

Aunty   ?

Gengis   You train your dog to kill the very birds in the trees

Aunty   Only Bedause he's hungwy . . .

Gengis Remind me, what is it just their little way of saying?

Aunty It's just their little way of saying that when the suffering is all too much it's time to stop for a few moments of reflection, a little sadness fills your heart, you can't go on, a tear comes to your eye, a sob mounts inside your head chest throat your eye, your vision blackens, a whisper from far away says 'someone, please if there is anyone, please forgive us'

Gengis But aunty why don't we all love each other any more? Has it always been like this?

Aunty I hope you don't think I'm old enough to remember?

Gengis Sometimes I get so depressed aunty

Aunty What you need is something to cheer you up

Gengis I know! The assizes! Justice!

Aunty That's right. It'll put the colour back in your cheeks

Gengis Bring in the first accused

Aunty The first accused is . . . Dickwits

Dickwits *is thrown onto the stage.*

Gengis Ah Dickwits, you bastard. What have you done to my people? You have ravaged them haven't you with your horrible claustrophobia. You've tried to hypnotise them but they didn't want you did they, they didn't fancy it. Well serve you right. They've turfed you out haven't they, but not before you degraded their palettes, they were gourmets once now they drink vinegar, even the babies. This is all down to your moral rectitude which you keep inviting everyone to examine. Well you've bent over once too often Dickwits, you've smiled sideways at the camera for the last time, you promised so much and delivered so little, you're on your way to the awards ceremony in the sky, see what the cherubim make of your inauguration speech and while you're at it you can cast my vote for me in the general election, then we'll see

what you smell like when you're laughing on the other side of
your face, counting your onions in your rotten borough. You
think I don't know, you think I don't care, well look at these
– real tears! Real tears mark you, not bought with your
socialist shilling, not banged out on your *Country Life* anvil
either, none of your cold steel here Charlie I can assure you,
none of your street carnivals and residents' committees
where I come from, we didn't submit it to a panel in my
comprehensive mate; playing fields? what bloomin' playing
fields? Just turn the page and read on. You're plain Jane,
Dicky boy, you're drab, right down to your wife's bangles
and your beads and your patent leather shoes and your
aerosol can. You've tidied up a bit too much is all I can say,
you've hoovered my favourite tree and strangled that little
Dicky bird with your endless bloody explanations. You want
a goal for tomorrow, I know you do my fairweather friend,
you may not recognise this court my fine fellow but we saw
YOU coming a mile off so there's no use in shrugging your
shoulders you're in there somewhere, by Christmas! You
won't be sitting on that wall for long with this morning's egg
on your face, don't worry about that, because you've been
bought. Oh didn't you think you were a retail item? Retail?
Retail. You're in the bloody clearance sale mate, you were
NEVER full price, you can call it priceless if you want but I
know what your posh customers call it on their way home
behind your back. You don't know what I'm referring to do
you, you don't know what I mean? It's all Greek to you isn't
it Charlie until you're sick of hearing it. Well, have you ever
wondered why? Help me down from here, I'm ready for my
operation. You perform it Dicky boy, because I know you
mean well and I'm grateful. I trust you, more than I'd trust a
friend. Bless you darling. Ok doctor I'm ready, get your
cross-saws out

Uncle *has returned with the necessary equipment.*

Trepanning begins.

Uncle   You see Dicky boy how you have won the royal
favour? He skirted around it now but there's no denying how

your muscular verse style and poetic diction has made a deep impression on his temporal lobe. This could be your opportunity to jog his memory

Dickwits *saws assiduously*.

Gengis (*speaking from the operating table*)   You can't hide it from me any longer, I have no kingdom left do I?

Uncle   Well, no . . .

Gengis   What darkness is this, what sadness fills the world? What have I done?

Uncle   One or two misjudged policies

Gengis   Tell me, wasn't I radical enough?

Uncle   Radical? You have chopped down to the roots and laid them bare

Aunty   The whole kingdom goes about without a stitch of clothing on its back. Not a fault is hidden

Uncle   Our wounds, all our sores

Aunty   . . . our blisters

Uncle   . . . our broken limbs

Aunty   . . . our torn eyelids, open beside the ditches

Uncle   The whole nation groans. There's no talk of a lack of radicalism

Aunty   No one says if only he were

Uncle   . . . more

Aunty   . . . radical

Uncle   No one

Aunty   . . . for they cannot speak

Uncle   Not a man among them can utter a word

Aunty   . . . enough to say −

Uncle   . . . more radical please

Aunty   No worry on that score

Gengis I don't know then . . .

Pause.

. . . perhaps I wasn't moderate enough

Aunty Of course you were. You have been moderate. In moderation

Uncle When it suits. Have you ever wanted to be moderate and not been?

Gengis No

Uncle There then moderate with a free will

Aunty Randomly moderate with a free hand

Uncle You have dispensed moderation with liberality, with a glad hand

Aunty Generously giving it away like gifts to your friends

Uncle Here friend, aunt, uncle here is a moderate gift, a gift given in moderation

Sawing continues, **Uncle** *slips out.*

Gengis Aunty, what is life all about?

Aunty That, nephew, is one of life's little mysteries

Gengis When will the mystery be solved?

Aunty Just before it's all over, when you will realise in the words of Dickwits here our national bard 'all is vanity'. In the face of death you will suddenly come over all sick and all scared and the allure of vain projects will pass away; Your books – you were never to read them, Your beautiful home – you were never to live in it, Your beautiful wife is a failure, Your favourite side of bacon in the pantry – covered in bile. It will all disappear

Gengis How do you know this aunty?

Aunty (*Whispers to him.*)

Gengis Is that why you so often smile secretly to yourself in that strange way?

Aunty (*does so*)   Perhaps

Gengis   I am pleased you have revealed these things to me aunty for I am now glad that this nation has been relieved of its its its —

Aunty   Its . . .

Gengis   . . . well everything

Aunty   Yes

Gengis   It is a good thing for the people because they are closer now to the meaning of life as revealed in the last moments of bitter painful nausea you described so well

Aunty   Thank you

Gengis   Keep a nation close to death and they will be close to life

Aunty   Yes, that is true. True words son. True, true words

Gengis   Unfortunately I don't think my people have benefitted from the terrible knowledge available to them

Aunty   Why not?

Gengis   Because they are all watching TV

Aunty   Bless them

Gengis   What is that clumping bumping sound?

Aunty   That musical marching?

Gengis   Yes that clomping and stomping

Aunty   That clippity cloppity?

Gengis   Yes that munching and crunching

Aunty   That hippity boppity?

Gengis   Yes that gnashing and grinding

Aunty   That skippity hoppity?

Gengis   Yes, that horrible noise!

Aunty   That's your uncle on his horse

Gengis   He must make a fine figure of a man. Aunty I have begun to notice a sublime look upon uncle's face. Perhaps he has discovered this enlightenment you speak of? And just now, well it must have been an apparition . . .

Aunty   Dreamy boy what did you see?

Gengis   Uncle, in a small room with what appeared to be . . . friends

Aunty   One of his workshops

Gengis   They were waving their arms in the air

Aunty   Just a warm-up dearie to prevent it all becoming too headbound.

Gengis   And when I asked what they were doing they turned at once and looked at me with strange hollow eyes

Aunty   They were probably just tired Gengis darling, your uncle is a terrible bore when he's helping people express themselves

Gengis   But aunty, there was a strange sense of evil in the room

Uncle *bursts in*.

Uncle   Yes and what's wrong with that you little squealer

Gengis   But uncle you were always so loving and caring

Uncle   Yes, and I shall love my people all the more once they have achieved the perfection I have planned for them

Gengis   It sounds wonderful. And what kind of perfection do you have in mind?

Uncle   In my dream kingdom supplicants line the streets. They fling money at you as you pass by, they lurk in every shop doorway and you are expected to hurl insults at them in return

Gengis   Is it easy to think of any?

Uncle   I usually cry out things like; nit-pickers! slow brains! limping fellows! ant-teasers! operatives! rotten vest!

Gengis   Are they pleased with these?

Uncle   I mention only a few of their favourites. I shall give animus to the pusillanimous, I shall make the crooked straight, where there is doubt I shall bring certainty, I shall never surrender

Gengis   How will you do all this uncle?

Uncle   Words

Gengis   Aha

Uncle   Yes it's all a matter of finding the right words

Gengis   And if that doesn't work?

Uncle   Then I have this big knobbledy stick

Gengis   Then you are bound to succeed. We are looking forward to the new order aren't we aunty?

Aunty   Yes dear

Gengis   But uncle, those strange leather boots

Uncle   Inside the top of my boots I have frogs for my enemies

Aunty   Urgh!

Uncle   Beware the man who denies my people the right to be very happy indeed

Gengis   Beware indeed

Uncle   Nothing but the best for my boys

Aunty   Quite right

Uncle   The quest awaits me

Gengis   And will you bring back food to feed the hungry babies?

Uncle   Better than that. I shall return at the head of a dark-browed column of the red-trimmed sons of judgement

Aunty   How thrilling and chilling

Gengis   But uncle I'm afraid, I like things as they are. I like being Gengis Khan, I like being the people's choice, I like taking everyone's money uncle, I like eating my little bowl of mumsmilk yoghurt of an evening, I like cheating in the elections and tricking the people and I like reading pornography in the bath, please don't spoil it

Uncle   Call that destiny, you money-grubbing degenerate, you low-minded sensualist pervert you? – (*Farts loudly.*)

Gengis   Uncle, you have farted

Uncle   Yes and let that be a warning to you. I shall expel all unnatural gases from the temple of my rectum until the whole of Europe stinks of my evacuation. I shall be free and you my lad will cough your Jewish lungs onto the table. (*Does so.*)

Gengis   Does this mean no World Cup?

Uncle   There will be one but my team will win or several million will live to regret it

The dog barks at him.

Tell that thing to shut up

Aunty   I can't sweetie he's excited by the noisome cloud still clinging to your slacks

Uncle   Then I shall silence his indignity. (*He stamps on the puppy's neck rendering it silent.*)

Aunty   Oh brute, brute, poor little doggie! You wicked man, you cruel man!

Uncle *marches out.*

Aunty   What a terrible change. Do you think we should have his throat cut to preserve world peace?

Gengis   No, he may want to buy something

Aunty   Sing us some gentle songs of suffering

Gengis   I've trained long and hard for this. Quick tie me up, lower me down, into the royal casket, this is no head cold. Don't you recognise the imperial goitre when you see it?

Aunty   Uncle! the razor-sharp incisions of our national poet have finally brought the tyrant to his last breath. Come back quick!

Uncle (*enters*)   Incredible. But shall the nation be denied one last goodbye?

Gengis   Alright, file them past but make it quick, the royal memories are washing over my consciousness. Gee whizz uncle, I was truly a pippin!

Uncle   *Bien sûr*

Gengis   Who are these people aunty?

Aunty   They are your subjects

Gengis   O their breaths are certainly no sweeter than when I came to the throne. Has it really all been in vain? Fuck damn my own stupid head for thinking up this idea, but I'll stick to it anyway. It will improve, where is Dickwits?

Dickwits   I'm sorry Your Highness, you were trepanned in good faith

Gengis   What part of my brain did they remove?

Dickwits   Your judgement Sire. And you'll find your backhand in tennis a good deal worse

Gengis   My way with women is intact I see

A worthy erection protrudes the blanket.

Dickwits   Ah the hangman's cudgel, as we call it Your Majesty

Gengis   Dicky, forgive me if I have been glib with you. I love you

Dickwits   You're fading fast Your Majesty. Should I pen a dying speech for you, your last words?

Gengis   Not on your life Dicky boy, even a farting corpse is more eloquent than the squeaking of your pips. Thanks but no thanks

Dickwits *bows and exits backwards.*

Gengis   You wait. Indira will come back one day and
you'll see. All this piffle-paffle, all this . . . politics! Indira is
beautiful, Indira is full of love, Indira has a temple of
humanity in her breast, Indira has long black hair and
smooth feet, and they are walking this way I can sense it

Aunty   And what do you think she'll make of you?

Gengis   She loves the people and they love her, she IS the
people. She is me. I am her. I am the people. I love her. I love
the people. I love myself

Uncle   It's all very well to come out with all this now I must
say. We haven't noticed you being very loving, have we?

Aunty   No

Uncle   We haven't noticed you kissing little babies and
having a joke with the pensioners. You're not exactly an
antivivisectionist are you, not exactly a vegan, not exactly a
supporter of freedom fighters on the street corners on a
Saturday morning with a bucket and a newspaper are you?

Gengis   I'm anti abortion

Aunty   You papist!

Gengis   Aha, so you'd like me to persecute Catholics now?

Uncle   NOT if they're Irish and wave the tricolour

Gengis   Damned if I can keep track of it

Uncle   Your frivolous attitude reduces politics to mere
flibber flabber, blibby blabby, gibber gabber

Gengis   It's your fault, you keep moving the goal posts

Uncle   Gengis, don't worry, just do as we do, say what we
say, we'll keep an eye on you

Gengis   Thanks uncle. I do try

Uncle   Alright good boy. His heart is in the right place

Aunty   It's all over the bloody place. What he needs is a
good kick in the cunt!

Uncle Alright aunty, we shall kick him there if he does it again

Aunty Hear? So just watch it

Uncle Isn't it sad to see a noble man sunk so low

Aunty And all because he tried to steal the march on his neighbour

Uncle But what a neighbour. People are saying he was not a man of total frankness regarding his relations with Indira

Aunty What treachery. So it was all a mirage

Uncle Remember how he went bankrupt soon after Indira left, and he shut up shop and disappeared? It transpires they were seen naked together on the banks of a river

Aunty And this is the sad-eyed goddess who so castigated poor Gengis for his little retailing peccadillo!

Uncle The very same, laughing in the moonlight with the sperm of her husband's rival swimming in her beautiful brown belly . . . So they say

Gengis When Indira comes I shall not ask her where she's been. Perhaps on her arrival she will give birth to the child of a fornicator and that child I shall wrap up in my arms and take it out and show my people; behold your deliverer! I shall call out to them, and they shall cry tears of joy

*　　*　　*

Day. Dawn. Night. Twilight. Day. Dawn. Night. Dawn. Twilight. Dawn. Day. Night.

Gengis Stop that

Aunty Well, what's next Plucky?

Gengis I shall merge the VD and cancer clinics. Better atmosphere and save money

Uncle Getting a little nervous about the approach of your beloved?

Gengis   She loves me uncle. She loves me. She loves me. ME. She loves me. ME ME ME

Uncle   If indeed she has the roving eye your days are surely numbered. You'd better get out quick in a getaway car

Gengis   Will you drive in that case uncle?

Uncle   Sorry son, cramp in my right hand, lassitude of my left

Gengis   Aunty darling, we'll drive off together. We'll stop off and get some shopping

Aunty   Can we can we can we really?

Gengis   Yes alright

Aunty   In my favourite mall, in my favourite shopping centre. I love the fountains, soft stream of light

Gengis   That's right aunty

Aunty   No fucking riff-raff there

Gengis   No

Aunty   Just shoppers, shopping shopping shopping shopping shopping shopping shopping shopping shopping

Gengis   Buying toys at Christmas most of them

Aunty   Yippee

Gengis   Big new duvets and sideboards

Aunty   Oooo

Gengis   Holidays

Aunty   Yippee

Gengis   Watches

Aunty   Watches!

Gengis   Lovely shoppers aunty, all waiting for you to come and join in

Aunty   Yippee

Gengis   Boom and bust boom and bust

Aunty   Yippee

Gengis   But watch out aunty, keep your hands to yourself

Aunty   Alright but if any police get in my way I'll fucking run them down

Gengis   Alright, that's ok

Aunty   I'll fucking go window-shopping with them on the bumper

Gengis (*sudden tears*)   It's no good I love her, I love her, I want my baby

Uncle   But she doesn't want you. Not since the days of the old shoponthecorner have you heard so much as a postcard. You see she has become interested in world affairs

Gengis   What? You mean she watches the news?

Uncle   Yes

Gengis   Then . . . she's well-informed

Uncle   Yes

Gengis   She knows what's going on?

Uncle   Yes she does and she reads the newspapers listens to the radio and looks at pictures, she's plugged in, she's got your number

Gengis   Bitch. I hate women like that

Uncle   You can't argue with progress

Gengis   They glance at *Titbits* and they think they're Bertolucci

Uncle   I know

Gengis   Ignorance is the bane of our age

Very long pause.

Most people are too dumb to realise that

Aunty   Ready sonny?

Gengis   It's no good, I can't go. Without her I am nothing

Aunty   She'll chop your little head off

Gengis   But first I shall taste the sweet sorrow of her rebuke. It is enough

Uncle   Then you will have to watch while I supply her with all the evidence against you

Gengis   Of course good kind uncle. You are a man of high ideals for which no sacrifice is too great, no treachery too low. I understand

Uncle   That's correct my boy. You shall be an egg in my omelette

Gengis   I shan't protest. If she says I am ambitious I shall say I am a man, if she says I was cruel, I shall say I loved only justice, if she says I was rash I shall say I am a poet at heart, if she says I was corrupt I shall say my duty has corrupted me, if she says I lied I shall say I love the truth too much to speak it, if she says I stole the lightbulbs I shall show her the palace of lights I built in her honour, if she says I betrayed my country I shall say I have no country for I am a child of the universe and anyone who believed otherwise was a sucker, if she says I betrayed my class I shall say my class has produced quite enough heroes for any epoch, if she says I betrayed my god I shall bless her, if she says I burnt books I shall show her my poems, if she says I trampled the blind and misled the lame, well, I am no doctor and neither is she, if she says I believe in an incorrect political analysis, I shall say the analysis believes me but I believe no one, if she says I am a tyrant I shall inform her that in the name of democracy all my policy decisions were taken by the cleaners, you'd better take it up with them, if she says I buggered aunty's doggie I shall say who can resist that sexy little pet and its waddle, and if she says I have no love I shall crash my cymbals and dance and sing and say YES! Let us speak of love!

Uncle   Dickwits has made himself visible through the portcullis

Gengis   What does he want?

Uncle   He can't say, he's unusually short of wind

Gengis   You'd better let him in or he'll say I'm playing hard to get

Dickwits *is thrown onto the stage.*

Gengis   Well, what is it?

Dickwits   The beautiful Indira is coming. She is walking across the desert at the head of a large force

Gengis   At last. Where are you going uncle?

Uncle   I'm going to meet her. Coming aunty?

Aunty   Yes, of course. Lovely girl

Gengis   It's me she wants

Uncle   Ok Gengis, one last request, before Indira comes

Gengis   One last request. Alright. A cigarette. No, two cigarettes. No a cigar

Uncle   It has been smoked, sorry

Gengis   Alright then, a meal

Uncle   The doggie has just eaten it I'm afraid

Gengis   Anything will do then

Uncle   Anything at all?

Gengis   Anything

Uncle   Name something

Gengis   A magazine

Uncle   Neither of us can reach

Gengis   Get me some money

Uncle   Money?

Gengis   Yes! Sell someone something

Uncle   There's nothing to sell that everyone hasn't already got

Gengis   Get me a merchant

Uncle   He's in his yacht

Gengis   Get me an architect

Uncle   He's in his rectangle

Gengis   Get me lions and tigers

Uncle   They are printed in a book

Gengis   Get me my philosopher

Uncle   He's crowded in his house

Gengis   Get me a museum

Uncle   It's underground

Gengis   Get me a park with fountains

Uncle   We've moved it outside town

Gengis   Get me an honest man to be my friend

Uncle   He's on tv

Gengis   Get me a beautiful girl

Uncle   She's unable

Gengis   Get me a smell

Uncle   It's on your fingers

Dickwits *puts the noose around his neck.*

Gengis   Get me a rope

Uncle   It's around your neck

Gengis   Get me a priest

Uncle   He's singing his song and clapping his hands

Gengis   Get me a blindfold

Uncle   It's nowhere to be seen

Gengis   Get me a tree

Uncle   There's only two planks

Dickwits *helps him onto a chair.*

Gengis   Get me a chair

Uncle   You're on it

Gengis   Get me a pardon

Uncle *gives silver to* **Dickwits** *who exits.*

Uncle   Can't hear you

Gengis   Get the hangman

Uncle   He's spending his guinea

Gengis   Get me Indira Indira Indira!

Uncle   She's right here, just coming

Gengis   Aunty, why do the men and women have no forgiveness in their hearts?

Aunty   Because it would burst their little hearts

Gengis   Aunty, why do their eyes fill with tears?

Aunty   They're thinking about the tears in their eyes like me what I do when I want to cry

Gengis   Aunty why do I never win a prize?

Aunty   Because there is no prize for you

Gengis   Aunty why does the wind blow?

Aunty   Because of those nasty weathermen

Gengis   Aunty, why has my tree fallen down?

Aunty   I cannot tell a lie, you cut it down with your big shiny axe of silver and gold you did you cut it down

Gengis   Aunty why are we out here in the terrible cold

Aunty   Because we are together holding hands

Gengis   Aunty, why can no one read the book?

Aunty   Upsidedowninsideoutbacktofront

Gengis   Aunty, why the biggest baboon?

Aunty   Because the kangaroo shoes jump higher

Gengis   Aunty, why so quiet in the sky?

Aunty   Because the crows are cawing elsewhere

Gengis   Aunty why the ragged soldier in his trench

Aunty   Because the shiny general on his horse

Gengis   Why the judge upon his bench?

Aunty   Because the rope around his neck

Gengis   Aunty, what happens when you plant a seed?

Aunty   The seed begins to grow

Gengis   What happens when the seed begins to grow?

Aunty   The clouds begin to fill with snow

Gengis   What happens when the snow begins to fall?

Aunty   The birdie sits upon the wall

Gengis   What happens when the wall begins to crack?

Aunty   The stick falls down upon your back

Gengis   What happens when my back begins to bleed?

Aunty   Then you are dead and dead indeed

Gengis   What happens when the cat's away?

Aunty   The mice begin to play

Aunty *tiptoes off.*

Gengis   Aunty, I'm frightened

Gengis *stands on the chair with the rope around his neck.*

Gate Theatre present the British Premiere of

Services

by Elfriede Jelinek

translated by Nick Grindell

cast

Claudia	Veronica Geary
Herbert	Richard Copestake
Waiter	Gregory Haiste
Moose	John Lightbody
Bear	Brian McGovern
Isolde	Jane Nash
Kurt	Philip Woodford

Director	Annie Siddons
Designer	Louise-Ann Wilson
Lighting Designer	Chris Clay
Sound Designer	Terry O'Leary
Video Designer	Matthew Gardiner
Production Manager	Vian Curtis
Stage Manager	Charlotte Hall
Deputy Stage Manager	Tara Soro
Mask Maker	Jane Henderson
Design Assistants	Ursula Prosser and Ali Taylor
Assistant Stage Manager	Tina Smith
Production Assistant	Jim Bishop

for the Biennale

Artistic Director	David Farr
Producer	Rose Garnett
Project Co-ordinator	Clare Goddard
Manager	Karen Hopkins
Literary Supervisor	Joy Lo Dico
Production Co-ordinator	Melissa Naylor
Press Officer	Rachel Stafford

Services is generously supported by the Austrian Institute.

Biographies

Chris Clay (Lighting Designer)

Theatre includes **Out There** (Riverside Studios), **Hamlet** (RNT Education/HMP Brixton), **Dance of Death, In Memoriam Fragments of an Elegy, Mystery Bruises** (Almeida Theatre), **The Tales of Fraülein Pullinger** (ETC Theatre), **Lady Julie** (Doc Theatre), **Voyage in the Dark** (White Bear). Opera includes **The Nightingale, The Rose** (Almeida Opera) and **Almeida Opera Concerts** (1993 and 1994).

Richard Copestake (Herbert)

Trained at Drama Studio, London. Theatre includes Fomin in **Katerina**, Marzio in **The Cenci** (Lyric Studio, Hammersmith), **The Trial** (European Stage Co., Young Vic), **Macbeth** (Northcott), **The Winter's Tale** (Plymouth), Jason in **Despoiled Shore** (Tabard), **Woyceck** (Edinburgh Fringe), **Ballad of Wolves** (Gate). Films include **Danny** (National Film Studio). Television includes **The Bill** (Thames).

Vian Curtis (Production Manager)

Resident Production Manager at the Gate. Trained at RADA. Theatre includes **Bloodknot, Don Juan Comes Back From the War** (Gate), **Heart and Sole** (Gilded Balloon/Newcastle Comedy Festival), **So You Think You're Funny!** (Gilded Balloon), **The Lottery Ticket** (BAC/Pleasance), carpenter for Hilton Productions and **Miss Julie** (New End Theatre, Hampstead).

Matthew Gardiner (Video Designer)

Training North Kensington Video and Drama Project: City and Guilds Video Production, 1995; Goldsmiths College, University of London, BSc Hons Psychology, 1993. Shot and produced documentary covering work of Mrs T Gardiner and Dr C Casserly psychologist and homoeopathic doctor in Romania and Hungary. Produced shorts (5 mins) at Goldsmiths and NKVDP. Researched 'blind date' phenomenon. Recent commissions include **Migrant Refugee Forum** and **Mark Elie Dance School** (both short documentaries).

Veronica Geary (Claudia)

Trained at the Poor School (1990–92) and Ecole Philippe Cautier (1993). Theatre includes Monica in **An Evening with Gary Lineker** by Arthur Smith (Vaudeville/No. 1 Tour/Assembly

Rooms), Colette in **Not Gods But Grants** by Paul McNeilly at the Traverse, Felicity in **Fragments of a Dream** by Tom Minter at the Riverside Studios, co-wrote and performed **One** and **It's not Funny** with Cathy Rogers (Edinburgh 1990). Shortlisted for the Guardian Student Award.

Nick Grindell (Translator)
Nick completed a degree in modern languages at Cambridge in 1992. Since then he has been living and working in Berlin as a translator and writer. His translation work includes work for scientific research institutes, theatres and most recently for other writers based at Berlin's 'Kulturfabrik', where the first public reading of his own work was held in November 1995. **Services** is his first major translation for the stage.

Gregory Haiste (Waiter)
Trained at Royal Scottish Academy of Music and Drama. Theatre includes Horse in **Europe** and Tom in **Away** (Traverse Theatre, Edinburgh), Peter in **The Railway Children**, Primus in RUR (Harrogate Theatre). Recently completed national tour of **It Runs in the Family**, playing Lionel Blair's bastard child. Spent many happy years at Manchester Youth Theatre where roles included Mephistopheles in **Faustus** and Satin in the **Lower Depths**. Film includes Iain in **Earth to Earth** (Beggars Belief Productions). Member of rock band **Godot was Shy**.

Charlotte Hall (Stage Manager)
Trained at Aberystwyth University. Theatre includes publicity team member for the National Student Theatre Company of Edinburgh, Company Manager for the National Student Theatre Company (Edinburgh '95), Production Manager for **Violent Night** (Absinthe Theatre Company, Man in the Moon), Deputy Stage Manager **Silverface** (Gate Theatre) and Stage Manager for **Dracula** (Steam Industry at BAC).

Jane Henderson (Mask Maker)
After a training in Fine Arts and a mottled career searching for the meaning of life, Jane realised it's much more fun to be serious about trivial things than to be trivial about serious things and now puts her talents to building puppets and props. She manages the famous singing chicken Edith Poulet! Recent work has included projects for the Puppet Centre Trust, Palace Theatre, Watford and a pop video for the Red Hot Chilli Peppers.

Elfriede Jelinek (Writer)
She is one of Austria's most acclaimed and controversial writers.
She was nominated *Theater Heute*'s Best Playwright of the year 1993
and declared the most important writer of her generation by
Süddeutsche Zeitung. Her work, which encompasses novels and
cultural criticism as well as theatre, has particularly focused on the
issues of lust, sexual power, and obsession. Her language is potent,
sexually charged and explosive. Her novels include **The Lovers**
(1975) and **Lust** (1989), which provoked extreme reaction because
of its horrifically candid portrayal of male sado-masochism.
Criticism includes **Totenauberg** (1991), a deconstruction of the
cult of Heidegger. Plays include **What Happened After Nora
Left Her Husband**, published by Methuen in **Plays by Women:
Ten**.

John Lightbody (Moose)
Trained at Drama Studio, London. Theatre includes Dodger in
Frost at Midnight (Chameleon Theatre Company, Prince
Theatre, Greenwich), Boudin in **1812** and Boy in **Vampry**
(Cuttlefish Theatre at Gulbenkian, Newcastle), The Clock in
Cinderella (Northern Stage at Newcastle Playhouse), Bobby
Shobean in **Bastardhead** (Beanbag Theatre Company,
Edinburgh Fringe). Left drama school in July.

Brian McGovern (Bear)
Trained at Bristol Old Vic Theatre School. Theatre includes Joe in
Brian Friel's **Lovers** (Bristol Old Vic), **The Oedipus Complex**
(Bristol Old Vic), **A Midsummer Night's Dream** (English
Touring Company), Clov in **Endgame** (Naked Theatre, Dublin),
Tommy in **Joyriders** (Birmingham Rep), **Silverface** and **Ballad
of Wolves** (Gate). Television includes Stew in **Casualty** (BBC)
and **The Hang of the Gael**. Film includes **Camera Attack – The
Facts** (Amotion Pictures). Radio includes Radio Rep, Bristol.

Jane Nash (Isolde)
Theatre includes **Pygmalion** (Nottingham Playhouse), **Square
Rounds** (RNT), **Fanny Hill**, **The Way of all Flesh** (Red Shift),
Much Ado, **Alice Through the Looking Glass**, **Good Person
of Szechwan** and **The Dream** (Duke's, Lancaster), **Measure
for Measure** (Young Vic). Television includes **The Bill**,
Chandler and Co and **Sleepers**. Radio includes **Blitzcat** and
Aliens (Radio 4).

Terry O'Leary (Sound Designer)
Television includes: post sync recording (dialogue effects) for BBC,
ITV and Channel 4 dramas, sound dubbing/mixing for quality
dramas and documentaries. Film includes: post sync recording and
assistant mixing for 35mm and 16mm feature films; everything
from student films to commercial cinema releases. Other: audio
experimentation, ie: audio/slide projects, record mixing and
atmospheres.

Ursula Prosser (Design Assistant)
Trained at Brighton University. BA Hons Fine Art Sculpture (June
1995). Work experience at Pebble Mill, Birmingham and RSC,
Stratford-upon-Avon. Theatre work: **Ballad of Wolves** (Gate).
Works and designs from Brighton Studio as a freelancer.

Annie Siddons (Director)
Trained at London University. Theatre includes: **Blazing New
World** (Etcetera) and **House** (Lyric Studio, Hammersmith);
Assistant Director on **Flora the Red Menace**, **Ruffian on the
Stair** and **Merchant of Venice** (Orange Tree).

Tina Smith (Assistant Stage Manager)
Trained at Mid-Kent College, National Diploma in Performing
Arts which included stage management, lighting, sound, set,
costume, directing, arts admin. and make-up. Theatre includes
numerous productions and one-off shows at the Central Theatre in
Chatham doing lighting, sound and crewing; properties and sound
fx at the Stag Theatre in Sevenoaks on **City of Angels** and follow-
spot at the Rochester Arts Festival in July 1995.

Tara Soro (Deputy Stage Manager)
Trained at Bennington College (USA), and BADA (London).
Theatre includes Costume Designer for **Charlie and the
Chocolate Factory** (Steamboat SPGS Children's Theatre,
USA), Stage Manager's Assistant for **A Quiet Little Wedding**
(Denver Centre Theatre for Performing Arts, USA), Director's
Assistant for **The Butterflies**, Costume Designer for **Ladies of
the Tower** (Lowell Whiteman School, USA) and Director's
Assistant for **Lend me a Tenor** (7th Street Playhouse, USA).

Ali Taylor (Design Assistant)
Trained at Nottingham Trent University, 1991–94. Theatre
includes Designer for **Thunder Rock** (Finborough), **Another
Saturday** (Roundabout TIE), **Stairway to the Stars** (Bradford

Festival), **Flora** (Oxfordshire Touring Theatre Company) and **Daughters of Copper Woman** (Noel Street Swimming Pool – site specific).

Louise-Ann Wilson (Designer)
Trained at Nottingham Trent University, BA Hons Theatre Design. Finalist on the Linbury Prize for Stage Design 1993. Theatre includes **How High is Up?** (Theatre Centre), **The Song from the Sea** and **All the Helicopter Night** (West Yorkshire Playhouse Schools Company), **Falling Angels** (Meeting Ground Theatre Company, Leicester Haymarket Studio and tour), **Natural Forces** and **The Edible City** (Humberside TIE), **Measure for Measure** (College Street Studio, Nottingham), **Hood in the Wood** (Roundabout TIE). Site specific and installation work includes **Rites Rules Wrongs**, Park Tunnel, Nottingham, **The Game**, based on **Miss Julie** by Strindberg, King David's Dungeon, Nottingham Castle, **Miss Julie** installation (Actors Touring Company).

Philip Woodford (Kurt)
Trained at Webber Douglas Academy. Theatre includes Horst in **Bent**, Garry Essendine in **Present Laughter**, Edgar in **King Lear**, George in **All My Sons**, Mr Hardcastle in **Love on the Dole**, **Salome** (Edinburgh Festival, 1992), **Cannibal Star** (Camden Studio, 1994), **A Suffering Colonel** (Bridge Lane, 1994), and **Brideshead Revisited** (National Tour, 1995). Television includes: **Respect** (Yorkshire TV). Short films include **Schlock Therapy** and **The Tickle**.

Services

or

They all do it

A Comedy

Elfriede Jelinek
Translation by Nick Grindell

Characters

Isolde *and* **Kurt** *(a middle-aged married couple)*
Claudia *and* **Herbert** *(a married couple, younger)*
A **Waiter**
A **Bear**
A **Moose**
Four **Swingers**
Two **Men**, *Two* **Women**
A costumed procession, including children
Two **Japanese Philosophy Students** *(must be the genuine article!)*

Translator's note:
'Swinger' is used here in the sense of 'promiscuous person'.
In recent years, terms such as 'Swinger Party' and 'Swinger
Club' have come into use in German. They refer to events
attended by couples primarily interested in casual sex.

Act One

A motorway service station. Large plate-glass front onto the car park, with further glass doors in the background, through which a sales area and the till can be seen. The interior is dirty and dimly lit, with litter lying around. At first glance the place seems to be abandoned. Semi-darkness. From outside, car radiators draw up to the window-panes, park or drive away again after a short time, like ships coming in to dock. Two women dressed in extremely sporting and obviously very expensive fashion come in, one younger, Claudia, the other older, Isolde. The elder of the women is too old and somewhat too fat for her training outfit. But the younger woman doesn't fit her clothes, which are near futuristic, either. They both come bursting in, look around them, wipe seats with paper handkerchiefs, etc.

Claudia   What an effort that was, getting them to stop precisely here.

Isolde   They wanted to keep driving. Like tall slim people with somewhere to go.

Claudia   It was stated quite clearly in the ad, wasn't it: Zwillingsgipfel Services? Animals were supposed to await us there in the midst of their hair.

Isolde   The way our husbands always get so excited when something out of the ordinary happens to them! Bringing a Mercedes to a standstill surely can't be such a problem, even in a suburban room.

Claudia   No mean feat, nonetheless. They don't understand in the slightest that one might want to eat something that comes in a colourful packet. As if Nature was planning an act of violence against them.

Isolde   They will find that the food here lacks the authentic touch of a chef. But the animals expressly stated this number of kilometres and gave the name Zwillingsgipfel. They wanted false names from us.

Claudia I mustn't forget, mine is Karin. I must learn it off by heart.

Isolde I lied with respect to my age, because one of the animals wrote that women over forty are no longer women. But I did so want to become acquainted with an animal.

Claudia An animal that travels may not have much choice of what to eat.

Isolde They're bound to be on tenterhooks, waiting to find out who's going to be putting the heat on them. The name I gave is Emma.

Claudia You have to have tried everything once. We're always so outrageously normal.

Isolde And what do we do if the animal doesn't think our bodies look good enough to eat?

Claudia In the ad it said they're looking for us so they can get their hot-rods into top gear.

Isolde Herbert and Kurt would never stand for that. The most they allow is the occasional solitary lock-in in the woods.

Claudia And the animals there don't want us.

Isolde Do you think they're already waiting down by the toilets like they said?

Claudia It's too early yet. I actually feel a bit scared. Especially with the men turning up in a minute to add to our problems.

Isolde You don't have to. You can still go back.

Claudia How am I ever supposed to discover the beast in me if I'm so afraid of strange animals?

Isolde Maybe they're already somewhere watching us to see if we match the pictures we sent of ourselves.

They peer around, look under the tables, throw away pieces of paper, etc.

Claudia   In that case they'll already have noticed that you sent a photo from your younger days. It said in the ad: two housewives from the suburbs.

Isolde   Right, Claudia, before the men come. In fifteen minutes, you say you have to go to where the Kaiser left a hole, to see a man about a dog.

Claudia   We've still got plenty of time, Isolde. Don't be nervous!

Isolde   But it has to be planned. No pain, no gain; I wrote that in my reply with my best regards. Only the photo wasn't me, I didn't even look like that in my younger days. Do you think the animal will notice? Or only when it's too late?

Claudia   The animal you've chosen will notice straight away that you're well past thirty. Anyone looking for women or couples in the Carinthia area of all places can't afford to be choosy. Just think of the suits they wear there. You've no need to be ashamed of your age.

Isolde   Just listening to you makes me itch under the expensive fabric of my being.

Claudia   Let's wait and see what brand of polyester these gentlemen of daytime leisure will be sporting, and how they're cut.

Isolde   It's all right for you to laugh. Your body still gives you something to be house-proud about.

Claudia   The animal stated what mattered to it most: openness!

Isolde   They don't need a spare key for me: they knock and fall straight in because the door's already open. Mind you, many organs are already in a state of disarray.

Claudia   Any old age. To please and tease.

Isolde   But we expect an assurance of total discretion from these life forms. We don't want any surprise meetings with the creatures in our own walk of life. That would be as awkward as vermin in the gusset of feeling.

Claudia Don't be silly! We can go right on with our waltz of life.

Isolde I don't want to be hermetically sealed any more. I want to be soiled. I want to scream out loud on the heathen nest of a fast breeder.

Claudia I was just thinking: my arse and thighs provide a fair amount of stretch material to get one's hands on.

Isolde One of the animals is supposed to be a gentleman from Murau who's into day trips. And more than a day is more than we have. We've got half an hour. At the outside.

Claudia The other animal is supposed to be an elegant man too. I'll make him confess just how far he wants to fly from the launching pad of his pent-up desires.

Isolde And you'll succumb to his urge.

Claudia And don't go saying your name, Isolde, whatever you do. You're always so rash.

Isolde I'll say what I've thought out: My body is his stable. When I open the door he turns up and wants to be put on a chain. Once one animal gets going the others all follow. Even if they haven't yet got wind of what's about to annihilate them.

The radiator grill of a large Mercedes draws up to the glass. Two men, one older, one younger, get out. They are perfectly got up as Niki Lauda and Alberto Tomba, i.e. extremely sharp sport gear, which doesn't fit the build of their bodies either. They are carrying a racing bike, which is minus one tyre, and a set of golf clubs. They are laden with luggage and come in puffing and panting.

Herbert Have you been to the toilet yet? We're not staying here, that's for sure. You can't see the countryside from here.

Claudia Sit down, darling! No, we won't be going to the toilet for another quarter of an hour.

Herbert But you were in such a hurry. You were in a hurry to powder your noses here and here only.

Kurt What kind of people have been discharging themselves here? Someone's vomited on the floor over there.

Herbert And on the floor over here it looks like somebody's been losing their body hair.

Kurt All those years of letting nothing but sport into one's body, where it can beat itself in a knockout, only to be molested by other people's droppings.

Herbert I put myself to the test because I want to be faster than my body. And then the scum of humanity appears on the scene, shoots a few goals and gets stuck in the net – like carrots strung up in front of me. But they don't make me get up and go.

Kurt We'll drink something that comes in bottles and then be on our way.

Claudia But I'm hungry.

Herbert You surely can't want to eat anything here. It's bad enough that there are at least five people trying at this very moment to steal our car or infect us with their badly educated salmonella.

From now on the men take turns at getting up, peering out the window and sitting back down again.

Kurt Degeneracy and financial ineptitude seduce people into stepping out before the world with their affairs. They meet up in places like this to leave us standing about with our clothes half buttoned-up.

Herbert We should give these aimless golf balls a good hiding before we send them back into their holes.

Kurt They'll run and hide all on their own. But not on foot! They're decorated with all kinds of nocturnal boredom.

Claudia Calm down!

Kurt I'd like to see your face when the car's gone!

Herbert Basically it's like this: we search for the truth and
we want to come out of our shells once we've found it. And
the poor are constantly trying to come in.

Kurt But they flake out as soon as they see the price-tags
we're awarding ourselves.

Herbert All this endless dirt which they even use to lay
their dining-tables.

Kurt The only outlook they have in the business world is
through the cellophane window in the envelopes.

Claudia Kurt, what are you driving at?

Herbert Do we really have to stay here?

Claudia Just until we've finished resting.

Kurt Must it be here? I can already hear the excuses
they'll make when they take the car: It fitted them better
than us! We were pulling it out of shape with our chests!

Herbert And anyway, the service here is non-existent.

Kurt Outside in the car park just now the people looking
at me seemed to have women's eyes. As if they had anything
to give. We give them furniture on credit so their lazy arses at
least have something soft to sit around on and all they can do
is make it hard again by coming all over the cushion covers
three or four times in quick succession without even trying.

Isolde Kurt, you're not at home now!

Kurt Thank God for that.

Claudia Instead of paying back the instalments, they
purchase TV sets so they can sit back and watch as likenesses
of themselves come bursting out of their children. Schools.
Churches. Hospitals.

Isolde Where are the simple pleasures?

Kurt Please yourself!

*Bright light is suddenly switched on. Obscene neon nudes of all colours
and in every position flash stroboscopically. Oversized advertizing
posters of the front pages of pornographic magazines are drawn up like*

the banners in church at Corpus Christi. They could also be carried around by sandwich men etc. Our four heroes act as if they are unaware of all this.

Claudia I think the Fadinger Natural Spring must be somewhere near here. It's nearly impossible to get still mineral water because people always want to go charging off into the wild blue yonder. Which is also why their bubbles burst so quickly.

Isolde We ought to be able to see the Hornjoch Calvary from here too.

The men jump up with her and peer out.

Claudia It's too foggy.

Kurt To me this landscape looks as if it has been left in the lurch by humankind. You can hear them knocking behind the walls. They want new cars so they can get back out into the open, because the ruined countryside is calling them of all people to the rescue.

Herbert Human beings who have to be quite literally kick-started into action.

Kurt I quite agree.

Herbert We too could have helped with the destruction of nature, but luckily we were travelling by motorail.

Kurt Why so rarely read a book? Why so rarely drink red wine?

Isolde Later on we'll be able to have been for a walk.

They all occupy themselves intensively with cleaning the seats and table with paper handkerchiefs.

Herbert Always having to wipe oneself clean of people! Why don't they keep themselves to themselves?

Kurt Like women, they'd be more likely to score if they dressed to thrill.

Herbert I can only speak for myself, but yesterday Claudia and I visited ourselves at home together.

Claudia It's true. And right to the end of visiting hours too! Then we'd done our time.

Kurt Would you all please let a generally audible call for help pass your lips if someone tries to steal the car!

He peers out, sits back down.

Isolde Listen here, Herbert and Claudia, your tacky teacup phrases are brimming over as if they were gold-rimmed. I'm only noticing it now that you're raising them to your lips for all to see.

Kurt (*sits back down*) No, false alarm. They're still sitting around over there at the entrance, as if they'd died prematurely, next to their overloaded vehicles, rubbing up against them like cats wanting to be let in. Only want to fill their water bottles from the tap. These strangers. Playfully, like animals, that's how they push themselves upon us. Meanwhile, the locals are venturing off to foreign parts by all means available.

Isolde Shouldn't we be going somewhere, Claudia?

Claudia (*looks at her watch*) Soon, Isolde! Have a look at the menu first to see what we're going to choose.

Kurt What *is* hate? What is love? Between them they've made this country greater than other countries. Because the people here have squeezed so much out of themselves. In order to fuel other people's fiery appetites with Mozart and their plastic reconstructions of all his rubbish.

Herbert Yes. People fed the flames.

Kurt A fine mess!

Isolde We'll go and buy ourselves something later, Kurt.

Kurt What do you want to buy yourself here? The best thing there is, the wonderful view of the Ruprechtskreuz, was brought about by Nature alone.

Claudia But perhaps outside we'll find a nice contact to stick our fingers in.

Isolde   Which will make us light up at long last.

Kurt   The only light around here is the reflection from the television, an aroused image for every moment.

Herbert   And over there, the TV room in case it rains. (*He points to a porno poster.*) In the crucifix niche where Jesus spends his eternal youth getting bored.

Kurt   Each to his own customized sporting contraption. Today the TV stars have taken over God's old role. What they bring forth drains away unused into each and every channel. No one is waiting to appear unto us in all His glory.

Herbert   Yes. The dregs of humanity are left languishing in front of the goggle box which enlarges their image for them.

Isolde   Kurt, you haven't darkened my door to give me cause for satisfaction for a long time. Have you thought about it?

Kurt   You must be going out of your mind! Have you noticed it too, Herbert, how women always want to be hauled out of the morass of their big, strong feelings. And by us of all people! They've worked out exactly how much we'll let their feelings cost us.

Herbert   I quite agree. Let's keep calm.

A buzzing becomes audible, as if from a swarm of bees. They all listen for a while. The bees quickly become angrier and angrier.

Herbert   Let's take no notice of the humdrum of the restless masses! Animals!

Kurt   All hell's broken loose out there. Inoffensive people like us don't incur penalties.

Herbert   Yes. A penalty. And the ball, booted by downtrodden hordes, flies into the goal.

Claudia   Could I expect a bit of understanding from you this evening, Herbert?

Herbert   Really, Claudia! Don't make me laugh! You want to be blown on riotous living and then you're all spent before you've had a chance to enjoy yourself. But even the small change is burning holes in *my* pocket.

Kurt   Yes, same here! Like softened laundry on the carpet.

Herbert   Why am I so hard, Claudia?

Claudia   I hadn't noticed you getting hard. (*Buzzing of bees.*)

Isolde   Look, (*She points to the porno poster.*) isn't that that sportswoman? Who's supposed to have been doping, what's her name again? Oh, who cares, anyway, her entire faked performance is etched as a greasy shimmer on her surfaces.

Claudia   She's got a skimpy bit of plastic between her legs, you can hardly see it. She probably knows no taboos other than those erected by medical science as a fence around her private possessions. Oh, if only we were that uncomplicated! Taking in substances, giving off subjects, how very fine!

Herbert   You can't want to be the same as her, Claudia!

Isolde   Oh yes she can. Claudia wants to be just the same.

Herbert   Freshly squeezed, or as good as freshly squeezed.

Claudia (*points to the porno poster. The bees buzz*)   According to the poster, one of the other things the area has to show for itself, apart from the Calvary, is an artificial lake several kilometres long which gives off electricity every day.

Herbert   Bet that's fun to watch! There's always got to be something to show for it, to make up for all the environmental damage, even when we make a tender grab at our partners.

Kurt   Credit where credit's due. They're forever grabbing at us too! From amidst their bushy hair.

Claudia   Our partners grab at us with realistic gripping hands until our motors are revved up to the mortality rate. That's how much I need Herbert, and that's just how Herbert needs me.

Herbert Is anyone ever going to take our order?

Buzzing of bees.

Kurt This sound sounds aroused. It makes me feel like I've looked absent-mindedly into the bottomless depths of another person once before. That was at a swimming pool with regard to a bathing beauty. Legs up to her armpits!

Herbert Indeed. A safe stronghold is our hormonal balance. So many things are firmly rooted in it.

Claudia I wouldn't exactly be in for a rough ride if you were my boss, would I, Herbert.

Isolde And you're never out putting yourself at risk either, are you, Kurt! Why are you never out? You don't even give my pain in the backside the occasional massage.

Kurt You've got a cream for that which butters you up more than I ever could.

Claudia But there's something inside me which wants to get out from under the skincare.

Herbert You've improved your backhand to make up for that though, haven't you. It takes someone who's seen you play tennis to notice just how much existence you actually have in you.

Claudia And just how quickly it would all like to escape me again. Yes, Herbert, sport is harder than you are, because there are rules to be learned by heart beforehand.

Kurt Take an example, Isolde, you and your classical music! Under your hairspray you're as stiff as a buttoned car bonnet. That's one habit you'll have to get out of.

Herbert The Fadinger Natural Spring is supposed to be a fountain of youth, even for tough cases. (*Buzzing.*)

Isolde Sometimes I dream of being in a stick up with a whole ton of spray.

Claudia   As for me, no preparation contains the amount of tenderness I require. Why, for instance, aren't *you* tender to me, Herbert?

Herbert   I can't believe I'm hearing this!

Kurt   You two always expect to be made to resonate by other people.

Herbert   No matter how much you're concertina'd in and out, the air goes back and forth without ever striking a chord. Your breathing is all that can be heard.

Kurt   This is a wonderful area! It would have been able to tell us something.

Herbert   Magnificent dark woods. You can spend weeks here crying out for another person to take a gulp from.

Isolde   Kurt, don't you think I'd look sweet upon the seat of an organ made for two?

Kurt   Yes, the organ in the old parish church. It says here in the brochure that the lake freezes over too.

Isolde   Hey! I'm a serious proposition!

Herbert   You can't even go into a sauna round here without being sized up by assorted glances. You must be as daft as you look after all to have wanted to park here, Claudia.

Isolde   Kurt, whenever I look for you in a pannelled room you're not there. I take up the chase, take what's mine, nothing. I'm well out of it. The thing lying dormant inside me that got up too late is my body, which I carry around with me just so that it can be put on a short leash like a dog.

Claudia   Yes, that's happened to me too. The body raises its head but then looks in a completely different direction.

Herbert   Why don't we let ourselves go for once? To a place where we can be moved?

Claudia   Sport! Just that kind of sport! That's where those cool, calm people with plans get together. With tans I mean.

Kurt   Will you be rally driving again this summer? Now, at last, we can lavish ourselves on half-forgotten peoples.

Herbert   The Iron Curtain is gone now. Isn't that reason enough for a celebration? We'll have to make sure we don't run out of unleaded petrol in Russia.

Isolde   I don't want to have to watch myself fall victim to the advancing years. I want to sprout creamy, puckered lips.

Kurt   Your words are shining like crazy!

Isolde   And you're the only one entitled to make withdrawals, Kurt.

Kurt   All that's left is alpine flora.

Claudia   Well, I'm going out now. Can you order me a juice, Herbert? The juices aren't going to start flowing on their own while I'm gone you know.

Herbert   Sometimes I think no one ever comes out of another person the wiser, due to having their eyes shut the whole time.

Kurt   A long passage, strangers have arrived with their sponge bags, opening up to anyone and everyone. Like dirty dressing-gowns. Revolting. That can't be what you want, Isolde!

Claudia   We've got it good in our insides, real cosy. Are you coming now, Isolde, or rather, 'Emma'?

They both look at their watches, get up, get out their sponge bags.

Isolde   One has obligations to one's body, Claudia, I mean, 'Karin'!

Claudia   Yes. The terror that prevails inside the body because we can't see in is made worse by the darkness outside.

Isolde   We see nothing but ourselves. But after a moment's panic the screen brightens and we can look in and watch our light entertainment channel.

Claudia   Us women have started something there all right!

They make signs to each other like in a pantomime. Very loud buzzing of bees.

Isolde (*almost inaudible*)   We must be off to where the Kaiser left a hole, to see a man about a dog.

Claudia   Yes. No pain, no brain. That's what it said in the ad, with best regards.

The women go out. The buzzing ceases abruptly. Upstage, the till and the sales area. The women stop to survey the wares, buy T-shirts etc. They are visible through the glass doors. A little show is being performed in total silence. Low-budget television ballet, all only visible through the glass doors. Women are lifted up and then dropped. A singer sings silently into a microphone. Etc. Downstage: The sloppily dressed **Waiter** *comes to the table and leans over* **Herbert** *and* **Kurt**, *who've been left behind alone.*

Waiter   What can I do you for?

Herbert *and* **Kurt** (*in unison*)   We've already had downhill and cross-country skiing fun today.

Waiter   Your lack of firmness could result in these women running away from you before you can say greased lightning. Say what you have to say before it's too late!

Herbert   They won't take lifts from strangers.

Kurt   They're just having a little think about which covering will keep their bodies from slipping. That's why they're buying T-shirts.

Herbert   They're buying. This ensures that the flowers flourish in excitement on their slopes. For the next few months.

Kurt   Because it'll take Mother Nature that long to deal with us having stormed her as a group.

Herbert   Indeed, our life is peculiar to us, we've chosen it ourselves.

Waiter   Yes, but God had the last laugh when He pickled your essence a poisonous seed in the glasses you drink. Bottoms up! You want to be off already, right? Time is more fun mirrored in the television and the papers. You tend to yourselves at regular intervals by having people stacked around you like pieces of furniture. You wish to get rid of these women again as fast as possible, the same way that you'd like to escape from Time on your skis.

Herbert We prefer to rent someone new in a dress. With nothing underneath. The faces of the most beautiful fuel-injection photo models change quicker than a ghost that gives up and throws down its shroud.

Waiter If you would just take a second to look: your wives are broadcasting the sex they've been blessed with from the rooftops. They're devastating their doughnuts. Hunger is at its greatest when no stomach is empty. I must remind you: not only the wildlife is wild. The shiny cycling shorts that kick out at the living are losing their allure. It will soon be night, when we are all possessed. Oh for a material that would lovingly embrace our tools! Sporting clothes leave little room for life's pleasures. But at the same time, sport is the only tool that can shift us. Women get undressed! A mound of plastic explosive which drives us between strange thighs! Yes, sport does nothing but wonders for the magnificent figure of a woman! Traced by the inexperienced little hands of artificial molecules. Almost as much suspense as a leotard. And underneath, some attractive secretary's piggy box, slot held open for our secretions, until the penny finally drops in her software. That's how they always do it! Take a look! Rounded, white paths which you've hardly begun to walk on when other airtight boxers come prancing towards you. Keep moving! In the wild, animals flee us, whereas here we are constantly searching and plumping for the animal in others. These women! They don't much like solitude because it forces them to hear their inner time bombs ticking all too loudly. Soon there's nothing left of them but their clothing, which is more elastic than Time. And they're off! Look!

Kurt We take a relaxed view of all this. They are no longer subject to youthful folly.

Herbert   Yes, you can say that for Claudia and Isolde. The hairs are standing up on their hot bonnets. We've got it made there.

Waiter   You should see how your ladies are tripping over their own shadows in their haste even as we speak! So that strangers can insert a programme of educational entertainment into them, a bomb so active that it's practically radioactive. These women aren't all there, but they always want to come! Any old age. Looks unimportant.

Herbert   We're in no danger of getting carried away by all your talk.

Kurt   As for Isolde, there's no way! The cover sheet of my bank account guards her against trespassers. The two of us appear to be coming along just nicely.

Herbert   The modest lake between Claudia's thighs, which took her years of hard work to dam up with Lycra, is hardly enough for the two of us. Any fish would soon be out of water. Indeed, Claudia and Isolde have become so tame they'd even eat fruit off the leash.

Kurt   I can't imagine they need a speedboat all of a sudden, just to get out of their depth again. Especially since they're so shallow you can almost stand up in them.

Waiter   You wanna bet?

Kurt   We are solid civilian vehicles. Anyone who sees our car believes us, including the police if it comes down to it.

Herbert   Waiter! Your pork pies will never get past our bullshit-proof vests.

Waiter   I suppose you think your Mister Muscle has polished them off to a T?

Herbert   I wouldn't go so far as to say that. But nonetheless, they *are* one of our favourite pleasure spots for outings, and we eat there too. They cook until they're done. Not a moment longer.

Waiter I reckon that if you were to try doing it with the curtains open you'd soon be needing the emergency toolkit. With other women you just might let your mayonnaise out into the open: maybe panty-hose under a trenchcoat, a bra, but they never stay long, do they? That is the very essence of the outing, that it doesn't last long. Until the sports round-up at the longest.

Kurt Come come, I'm not like that! Of course I'm interested in making my little man more trusting, but just not with my wife who's been raising him for years. With them he behaves himself and nods approvingly.

Herbert We are not averse to raising our standards if needs be. Standard French, ancient Greek, you name it. Anywhere's good enough for me to dump the junk out of my trousers, still spattered here and there with human material in the process of becoming. Yes, this is the stuff that world champions are made of! We've got what it takes!

Kurt As Herbert says. We've got it in us. We won't let simple eyes simply dismiss us.

Herbert We pass straight through them like food.

Someone walks past and casually steals the bicycle without looking. No one notices.

Waiter If you were to approach your wives in disguise, gentlemen, they'd even do it with you!

Herbert Possible, but not topical. Impossible. Inconceivable.

Kurt They've got competition from women in suspenders. They know this and they keep quiet.

Herbert We alone make them take leave of their senses. And we worked hard for our own senses too, so that now they can work for us. We didn't steal them.

Kurt Not even once!

Waiter Big deal. Now you've opened the can of worms where Nature has been keeping Time you'll just have to eat it all up. The possibilities are all maturing in their patchwork beds, playing with their members, and snapping out at us. Video, for example, is the most powerful image of all the human behaviour we could ever act out for women, or they for us: Three cheers! Hip, hip! You, gentlemen, are of course decent, still waters, but your wives want to make waves with you until their feelings are totally bottled up and until yours are twisted for good. I can't help feeling sorry for you! How tightly the rut holds you! And all the time the crackling sounds of mastication and shopping! Such anger! And all because someone turned on the waterworks! It gushes skywards, that's what women want. What a fuss they make when a storm breaks in their teacup. Thanks a million! That's all we needed! No, hold on, that wasn't it yet. First you are required to give head and have your knobs polished. You often ejaculate at this point and then get an earful because all your reserves have been used up, am I right?

Herbert   I've long since lost count. The forfeit is a discussion.

Kurt   With my one free hand I have often had to operate one of Isolde's gadgets.

Waiter   The thoroughness of women is enough to scare one stiff. They're always thinking about life as a whole rather than about the glasses and crockery they're delivered with. Your wives are obviously the type of women who make such an entity of their sex that it leaves no space for second parties.

Herbert   They've always had a pretty firm grip on us. So we don't really need to get to grips with them.

Kurt   Isolde is up to her ears in all the things she wants to do. But she never does them because she prefers talking about it.

Herbert   Yes, they give us plenty of words, but none that we can come to terms with.

Kurt   They speak as if they had to dismantle themselves brick by brick.

All of a sudden, nifty swingers are chasing each other through the room in various states of undress.

A Man (*in underpants, half out of breath, almost inaudible*) Offer them a wonderful view of at least twenty-three point seven centimetres and they just run away like kids from a spanking. Have a headache. And all that sighing nonetheless! And it's always got bones in. And no one's ever ready for it.

One of the party steals the golf clubs. No one notices.

Waiter May I recommend several small alterations: have the courage to be different for once! Simple false beards have been known to make the creatures of the night change their tune by at least a semitone. The stupid being whose glory hole you've been breathing life into for years won't recognize you! Show your wives a thing or two! They will throw a brief tantrum at their spoons and saucers in the kitchen, but then they'll be good girls and adopt all the positions Mother Nature has put on the vacancies page for them. Only to find them all taken because Mother Nature favours the young, whom she can show the way out of the cradle and into the pop concert.

Herbert How can a nice, slim, well-endowed guy like me avoid being recognized immediately? Some things simply can't be covered up. They're just too obvious.

Kurt I'm also sure to be recognized, on account of my tiny tanga.

Waiter It's all a matter of trying to look unfamiliar. That shouldn't be difficult seeing as it's years since your wives last took a closer look at you. Once the silence starts ringing shrilly in their organs they're bound to answer the call. And when they lift the receiver they'll be in the grip of your infectious, love-filled vocal chords. It is quite possible that your gruesome, ever-present appearances will then be quite unfamiliar and new to them, or as good as new.

A merry foursome sit down at the next table. They are already almost undressed. They laugh, maybe only fragments of their speech can be heard, due to the soothing muzak which is playing. The **Waiter** *leans* *over* **Kurt** *and* **Herbert**, *gives them the menu and recommends something, but both of them have eyes only for the four people at the next table.*

Man 1   Where did you park then?

Woman 2   Right next to the conveniences. It's better if we can go straight in. Wherever there's groups of people it's soon a tight squeeze.

Man 1   Just you make sure you're tight yourself! And anyway, is this huge clitoris of yours you were telling me about in the car really a gift from Venus? Sounds like pure hard work to me.

Woman 2   You make it sound like I'm an animal. At least animals can be kick started into action.

Man 2   In my body the extras are already built in. In my car I had to pay extra.

Man 1   Hardcore! I'm submissive and I'm looking for used knickers and tights by Wolford.

Woman 1   Just a second and you can have mine!

She takes off her tights under the table and gives them to **Man 1**. *He sniffs them and throws them in the waste bin.*

Man 1   Wrong brand. They're not made of Herculon!

Woman 2   Do you really think I should buy my husband a nozzle for his little jet?

Woman 1   Last time there was a sales rep there who explained how it works. You want to know if you should buy him a vacuum pump for his small penis?

Woman 2   It would put more lead in his pencil than those political phone-ins on TV.

Man 1   There are always women coming along who get behind when it comes to ancient and middle Greek because they haven't learned any foreign languages. But I beat a hasty retreat if my knocking isn't answered, at every single door, I tell you. Then you see me disappear behind the bushes. I'm only game for everything, not just for a selection. And even then, any selection there was definitely wouldn't include you.

Woman 2 (*to* **Woman 1**) The size and staying-power of his penis are not ideal. One looks down the barrel and asks oneself, is this thing loaded or not?

Woman 1 I'm afraid that handling the equipment is not altogether without its hazards.

Woman 2 Like anything one has not altogether mastered.

Woman 1 (*to* **Man 1**) I'll have to disappoint you there. I'll have none of your Greek culture in my back yard. I'm more into DIY-fun.

Man 2 What do you need us for then? I'm looking for a woman who doesn't always wake the neighbours with her cries of anticipation when I'm getting down to some serious work with my little man. She should love him. But the grown-ups should tell him off for getting dirty.

He opens his briefcase and pulls out a nappy and a light-blue romper suit, extra large of course, which he pulls on with some effort over his Y-fronts.

Man 2 And anyway, that wasn't you on the photo!

Woman 1 That was my sister. She can't come today, she had a prior engagement.

Man 2 I would have preferred your sister. I've already seen her as my mother in a dream.

Woman 1 But you could come along with me for the ride.

Man 2 I wouldn't even want to travel in the same car as you.

Woman 2 You can only use *me* under a fine veil of rain where your lonely parts will shiver at the very thought of the frigidity of the only party you've chosen to remain faithful to for years! So there!

Man 1   Erotically speaking, children are the only competition for women. So you are right to want to be a child. But not with me!

Man 2   I've had enough of stopping after just one squirt. The child squeals when it's impaled on a love-skewer. I'm so looking forward to it!

Man 1   Just you wait until my bowel control goes to pot, even though I only play in the regional league.

Woman 2   But I've got photos and videos and my own love nest to go with them.

Man 1   Let's see what you look like on the photos! Then we'll be able to see if it's any match for the real thing.

They put their heads together and look at photos, occasionally holding a slide up to the light. The man-child is ready and flexes his body in the romper suit like a jogger. They whisper among themselves a little more and then get up and leave together.

Waiter   Did you hear that? How lightly they take to their leisure? Whereas it takes your wives weeks just to forget an unbecoming hair-do, am I right?

Herbert   You mean the flesh must arise every day?

Kurt   You mean one can feel like a God in a stranger's body? One can kick down the door to a room where entry is forbidden? And the body ends up better off than last time? Or doesn't get off at all due to fatigue?

Waiter   Don't go wasting your lifetime unnecessarily! The extra-lightweight Lycra tights which had you tied to the wheel like butterflies will crumble away! Nature has the same thing up its sleeve for your faces! And the skimpy bit of elastic between your wives' legs? Get the hell out! Surely you can muster up two hundred schillings and a bottle of Babycham, or some other bubbly. Our car park will soon put you in a whole new frame of mind! A moment's silence in memory of your car, but not a moment longer!

Kurt   A memento, you mean?

Waiter Available in the foyer!

Herbert Let's give it a go. But we're worried that pros get disqualified.

Kurt But we don't want any experiments with our valves, they might go wrong. Why don't we start by trying it on to see if we get a result up front?

Waiter That's the right spirit. Many VIPs of bygone eras couldn't have done without it. Please gentlemen, step outside, where you will find our programme of refreshments. Sympathy is everything. It cannot be replaced by mundane anal games, just you remember that!

He tips food onto the table with gusto, then pisses over it in a high arc and leaves.

*The two men, **Kurt** and **Herbert**, lower their heads to the table and slurp up the food.*

Kurt We've let ourselves in for something there! Herbert, your narrow gauge railway leads you into a woman and all of a sudden she happens all over you before your signal's even gone up! We're just not used to that kind of thing any more! Her silence is roaring and then, as women will, she starts talking about her hobbies, which allegedly correspond exactly with your own: sport, culture, art. But her pussy just won't start purring. Too much choke. Tough titty.

Herbert I've heard it all before. The next thing you know she's calling out my name while her batter is still sizzling on my wick! It's two days since she got the hots and she hasn't said a word.

Kurt Women do nothing but their own thing.

Herbert Which they consider to be of the utmost gravity. Because they turn out human beings.

Kurt Nature requires plenty of moisture, it's as simple as that.

Someone walks by and steals the rest of their baggage, as if in passing. He is not paid any attention.

Kurt I've been doing it for so many years. Again and again Isolde steps into a gloomy village which she's just spent hours describing to me. The door to an apartment is unlocked. Isolde stands rigid up against the wall. Won't take my weapon. Unpleasant. Like a waiter suddenly vomiting all over you.

Herbert How they descend upon one in the darkness! We at least have our car to measure up to.

Kurt The car is a measure of what we are. (*Jumps up, peers out, sits back down.*)

Herbert Its proportions are to scale. Is it still there?

Kurt Yes. Or on wash-day. She won't let the housekeeper do my laundry, she does that herself. A token of love. I always hear her asking whether things are white or coloured. She can't even see *that* without instructions. But she still thinks she knows my innermost self.

Herbert And whenever we enter the dark silence of the senses we notice how unpleasantly loud they can become.

Kurt In a hotel room a woman once said to me, in English, that it couldn't have been me who pierced the night with a scream.

Herbert It's about time a lower abdomen curled itself around us like a foetus.

Kurt As if our misdemeanours were being written down somewhere. We can hardly even believe ourselves!

Herbert There are Nina and Barbara again, the ones from the fitness centre. Silence has reigned between us for years because we always made a detour via sport and got whacked.

Now the grand entrance of the animals: two gigantic animal-men come in, like totems, everyone stares at them. Only **Kurt** *and* **Herbert** *continue to peer out at the car park, keeping watch on their car. After a while they take out a pocket chess set and begin to play. The animals are enormous, they're wearing platform shoes. The* **Bear** *is padded out,* *very fat. The* **Moose** *is very tall and thin. They must seem dangerous, like idols, but speak in the quietest conversational tone. The carrying-on in the background, behind the glass doors, becomes more turbulent.*

Moose   Can we sit here?

Bear   Looks like it. Were you promised the power of language too? And have you been to pick it up yet?

Moose   Yes. I speak out because there's simply too much pent up inside me. I make myself by speaking. An awful situation!

Bear   You're making a good job of it, if I might say so.

Moose   Would you please tell us your profession? Accompanied by a characteristic hand gesture?

Bear   I'm a sales rep for construction machinery of EC origin. Who'd have thought that anyone would ever draw up something so unreal and then actually try to build on it? Most of the time I travel abroad, Hungary, Poland, in countries whose names one can no longer remember, and in the new Länder of the old Federation.

Moose   How nice of these charming countries to have waited so long, just for us.

Bear   For us to come and plant them with our particular brand of *joie de vivre* in their very own home soil.

Moose   I'm a sales rep too, but for office machinery. Fun and fucky-fucky! Fun and fucky-fucky!

Bear   If speech can be called a human achievement, then these wonderful machines are practically superhuman. Who devised them? Women in particular are forever delving into themselves with language and coming up empty handed.

Moose   Yes, there's just no end to the inner life. With machines, on the other hand, one can transcend oneself.

Bear   Your performance as a body is magnificent!

Moose   Your body performs magnificently on the market!

Bear   These countries we export ourselves to can look back on a dead past. Some people would love to do that: ejaculate and then stop dead.

Moose   The West began paying them lip-service and wagging its tongue. That was a mistake.

Bear   After that they took themselves into their own hands. Now they can't keep themselves to themselves. All those movements, just to give themselves away to the first bidder.

Moose   And then we come to light. Well-built and a better vintage.

Bear   If they have any sense they'll stick to being the shopping paradise they are at the moment. Where every joke announces that they now have a good constitution.

Moose   Tootsy frootsy ice cream!

Bear   My company fits them out with facilities they've never had before so they can squeeze out those last few drops which we haven't managed to extract from them.

Moose   A new recreation room for their essence, which sits around in station cafés, throws its weight around, or lets others throw it on the rubbish dump. Villages and towns are measured out in advance just so that the evil essence has a room to shower in at last.

Bear   On the radio people come across as incomprehensible voices. Loudspeakers breathe in apartments. And anyone who volunteered can now be stored away as Time in the mind of a listener. Yes, or even become a listener who consciously has favourite programmes. Every individual is indifferent.

Moose   We're speaking! We're speaking!

Bear   We animals are different from humans.

Moose   I demand sex on a daily basis. Is that a mere error or an actual vice?

Bear   Tightening its grip, bearing down on us noisily like a juggernaut, it lets us ride in the cab for a stretch, and then leaves us in its wake. Animals sometimes get run over.

Moose   What happens? The housewife's *raison d'être* is to have a meteoric impact on the other housewives in the supermarket. She then lies down happily in the resulting crater. The animal comes to her and rings three times. She takes off her knickers. In cases where so many reasons for procreation are multiplying one should go forth and make oneself as comfortable as possible.

Bear   In Czechoslovakia someone offered me their thirteen-year-old daughter in exchange for a second-hand dot matrix printer. She had TB. These people have wasted their nature in unbelievable ways, on themselves of all people.

Moose   Their most competent representatives are now moving in on foreign countries as if they were cake shops. So they can stuff themselves and add extra lashings of whipped cream to the thrashings the inhabitants get. The cherries glow. Then they get tanked up while mounting the guard on their fresh-baked tarts.

Bear   I'm just going to assault my costume so I can come out of my shell quicker. (*Opens the zip at the front.*)

Moose   Why must we always dress according to the latest fashion? It's like a compulsion. (*Opens his zip too.*)

Bear   So that we don't die out in the middle of the forest. Children at the zoo would cry.

Moose   We point downwards out of our trousers. Is no one around here going to take pity on us?

A Tupperware stripper comes on stage and strips. **Moose** *and* **Bear** *nestle up to her garments and masturbate discretely.*

Moose   Question: why am I staying so dry today? Why only admire women from the safety of the opposite kerb?

Bear   Visit dingy suburban bars where women do themselves harm.

Moose   The air which has been made so bad by the industriousness of humans pushes a woman's skin to the verge of her face. Bacteria have found their way past the fillings in her teeth. Underneath, a presence which breaks forth displeasingly when she speaks. Stink!

Bear   A pleasant presence is absent.

Moose   Super! Tootsy frootsy ice cream! Snow and the evening chorus prompt people to jump start each other. Human bodies are the only ones with fuel to spare for home cooking.

Bear   Attached men are considerably looser.

Moose   Come out of their shells – awful presence!

Bear   A man always wants to sprinkle as if he was in the garden. But all he has is a one-room flat with a philodendron.

Moose   I once gave a woman an electric toothbrush as a present. She slipped while using it and her brains went walkies. Where to? To follow a calling.

Bear   You didn't have to go and become a murderer.

Moose   How often does a body die because something didn't stay where it was supposed to be?

Bear   I've seen several women die because something got into them that wasn't supposed to be there.

Moose   Excellent!

Bear   Like many of our counterparts, all you want is to reach the parts other counterparts can't reach, am I right?

Moose   The best results are obtained by barging into the miserable relationships of strangers and forcing the sprinkler on someone who would rather be left alone. It's so long since we went into the forest to scare people by bellowing.

Bear   Excellent! A woman whose eyes theoretically give you the thumbs down!

Moose   Precisely. I pay extra to be treated like a baby. That kind of intimacy is like a blanket of Nivea over the whole of one's upper crust. It sets me up nicely for domestic life, careering round the tiny patch of grass in the front garden. And the wife either comes home completely saturated or doesn't come home at all.

Bear   She'll only cut the mustard with me by making-believe she's never had custard in her muff before.

Moose   Now you're talking!

Bear   Women don't even care about our size because they usually take it lying down. We are bad-mannered, rough-cut lads and we bring death in our fur coats.

Moose   It has been known for humans to come when we called for women.

Bear   Excellent!

Moose   Excellent! Not like us! Not like us! Not with us!

The two men at the next table, **Kurt** *and* **Herbert,** *have only been playing half-heartedly the whole time and stealing glances. They now exchange a few whispered words, get up and squeeze in next to* **Bear** *and* **Moose** *at the table.*

Herbert   Excuse us. With your permission. Now that your sap is rising we can ask a question.

Bear   Let's be having the second stanza!

Kurt   What about that poison called feeling? I'm a great believer!

Moose   We are at pains to remain gentle.

Bear   You look like someone who wanders around with a guitar on his back, unsheathed and oven-ready, but no one plucks at his instrument.

Moose   Because a face like yours needs to be seen front on to be seen at all.

Bear   You cook on such a low flame that nobody notices you're cooking at all. You have to let things boil right up to the rim.

Moose Only then can you besmirch people. Flood them with minestrone soup for all I care. *My* liquid refreshment is made of nothing but fresh milk.

Kurt Some bodies triumph through love.

Bear Toilet games! Toilet games!

Moose There you are, still dangling from some human, helpless, claws and paws spread sail-like above them, and then the natives hang you right up alongside! The brutality of it! Up against the wall as a trophy! So much for love. Pah!

Bear Go squeeze some juice out of yourself, you lemon!

Moose Feelings have to be paid for in one little form or another, which then carries your imprint for all eternity even if you would have become much larger in the meantime.

Bear The only adventures a human should know are slalom, giant slalom and Super-G.

Moose But not us! The annoying thing about unrestrained people is that they never know where to go.

Kurt We accept all that with due respect as long as our wives, who have a right to themselves and to their daily make-up, don't become emotionally derailed. We spent many years patiently building this model railway for them in our spare time.

Herbert We've often had to be called in to act as heavy-duty bulldozers and lift them back onto the still-steaming track which we'd marked out for them, admittedly rather too faintly, in yellow.

Kurt Which we've marked out for them on earth and in the universe: that's to say, universally.

Herbert And then all of a sudden we noticed that although we'd fastened them to us securely, their bodies had developed a dangerous leaning towards us.

Kurt Despite the fact that we haven't the slightest inclination towards them.

Moose   Technically impossible. That which is bound together always leans in the same direction.

Bear   I'll vouch for that.

Moose   I'll trample them to the ground, if you so desire.

Bear   The natural side of me agrees and eats them up immediately. A lamb can stamp out a fire if only it wants to. Better to clobber the lamb in good time!

Kurt   As for those two over-garnished apples, Isolde and Claudia, who scream under their nighties, we've already eaten them all too often, right down to the stalk. But we've never been able to digest them properly.

Herbert   I quite agree.

Kurt   We are people who have to reckon with Time, and it's nearly eight o'clock.

Herbert   You see, my good animals, what do lovers do? Gaze into each other's eyes to aid their spiritual cross-fertilization and want to know each other down to the very last detail so that even that can be dragged out again in the dying process.

Kurt   Our path is strewn with tickets for cinemas, concerts and theatres. We are encircled by scraps of paper.

Herbert   This paper-chasing after the animal in us is an expensive business. And then there's the breath we waste when we undress in front of each other under the sporting pretext. There's more to be seen at any poolside where the suntan lotion drips from the grasses.

Kurt   At least you are animals already, dear presences and meals!

Bear   Wouldn't it be nice to be a beer tent so as to be abandoned among many others? So as not to be the only one who's humiliated?

Kurt   Do you animals not want to encounter anything other than members of your own species?

Bear   The eating habits of weaker species aren't much different.

Herbert   But in love every single person is oneself! One makes oneself comfortable within the partner's sporting confines.

Kurt   I've noticed that in love one loses one's essence and rots away.

Bear   Hikers are afraid of us. That's what humanity has come to.

Moose   In the wild, we often observe how people who have fed themselves on nothing but junk simply throw away their still-curvaceous wives in the curves of life's cross-country ski route. And we, Nature's police, then have to eat them up. But I prefer berries.

Kurt   It's a pity we severed our ties with Nature, isn't it?

Moose   Yes, us and Nature simply have to stick together.

Kurt   You two cut a curious figure. We should make a plaster cast of it to see if we'd even make remotely plausible animals.

Herbert   We've never seen anyone like you before. You must be good, quite simply because if you weren't then we'd be done for in ten minutes flat. Just because you decided to lift a finger. Yes, be good sports, or at least give us a sporting chance!

Bear   It sure is fun. Wherever us animals get together a gawping crowd forms which always contains someone who wants to rip us up into bloody shreds.

Moose   That person has to be singled out in good time.

Bear   Born to delight the world and then immediately done away with again.

Herbert   That all sounds very good. Listen, don't you want to swap costumes with us? So that our wives take a closer look at us again at long last?

Kurt   What fun it would be! If we were destructive and unrestrained. Biting and gorging our way through the rows of seats in the cinema, with fisticuffs!

Herbert   Yes. If you lend us your classic chaos costumes we'll pay!

Kurt   Yes, we'll pay for everything, all inclusive.

Herbert   Hand over the bear and the moose to us. Then we can consume our wives differently for once.

Kurt   As predators.

Bear   We have a *rendez-vous* here with a so-called Karin and a certain Emma. You could say that our role here is that of a rude noise about to come screeching out. Music! And then seize flesh as our property!

Moose   We don't really want to go without our nice, new *rendez-vous*.

Bear   Now is perhaps the moment to mention that the women we are planning on meeting and eating have lied with respect to their age.

Moose   One of the photos they sent was twenty years old! Animals may not have much stuffing between their ears but one shouldn't take them for idiots.

Bear   He's right you know.

Moose   Maybe age is a danger to humans because something can escape them unnoticed and be lost forever.

Bear   Although I don't quite see what they still need it for apart from maybe to pad out their trousers.

Moose   You really want to be a good-natured animal like me? The goo-goo eyes on paper plates which I prepared earlier are waiting inside me ready to be served up.

Bear   I'd rather go round and take the chicks by stealth. In me, Nature carries on fighting its old battles with new, lethal weapons.

Kurt   Something different, just once.

Herbert   Make that twice.

Moose   We have a *rendez-vous* here as Bear and Moose with two women from Bruck an der Mur and Karpfenberg respectively. That's what they claim anyway, but it's sure not to be true.

Bear   They just don't want us to be able to follow them home and bag the remaining parts of their bodies.

Moose   They imagine that when we are on fire for sheer love they can extinguish us with blows. Heard it all before.

Bear   They want to walk all over us. Instead of fanning us still higher. Restlessly pacing up and down a room instead of getting the feel of claws breathing down their neck, heard it all before.

Moose   What the hell, let's just leave ourselves a little way behind! We'll soon catch ourselves up again!

Both animals shrug their shoulders indifferently and snuggle against their costumes. They open the zips and step out. One can see, however, that **Moose** *and* **Bear** *are wearing another moose and bear costume underneath, two costumes one inside the other, so to speak. The moose's antlers are made of foam rubber and flop out from under the headset like a jack-in-the-box, shaped like a kind of winged TV aerial. The two men,* **Herbert** *and* **Kurt***, don't seem overly surprised by this. They take off their sport outfits and put on the animal costumes. However: the bear costume is far too large in height and breadth, the same goes for the moose costume, very tall but also very tight! The men do battle with the costumes. In the meantime, a little stripping interlude! Exit* **Kurt** *and* **Herbert***, tripping over the costumes and nearly falling. Curtain.*

Act Two

Entrance area of a large motorway service station's women's toilet. Many cubicles next to each other. Mirrors etc. Everything desolate, dirty, covered in graffiti. The women sitting on the toilet in adjacent cubicles. They have left the doors open.

Waiter's voice (*from a loudspeaker, over quiet muzak*)   Ladies, your husbands are so spoilt for choice they're exhausted! Make your own choice! The fact is that these countless options drive small-town people to their city limits. Beside you, in front of you and behind you are those people with dripping pricks and labia whom you've sought and found. One hundred per cent discretion and healthiness is expected! Have the bottles you were given at the counter and the exact money ready! The little sex messenger beside you has spent the whole season getting puffed up on winter sports. Now, ladies, he's going to plumb new depths and pour forth into you. The camera wants to see this! Position yourselves over the bottles you've received! Please open the doors a little wider (*The women do this.*) so that the camera can see how you take a leak before carrying on. Your secretions will be labelled *Golden Delicious* and drunk by our contestants during the final showdown. Jaws hit the floor, the crowd goes wild. A wave of happiness surges towards us. A meeting of the mindless which shows just how much ill-taste and blindness our biorhythms have inflicted upon us.

Isolde   Although I was open to feelings from the outset, I'm now having trouble peeing into this narrow bottleneck. I'm no sportswoman. I'm not that winning.

Claudia   It's perfectly OK for a woman to realize that she's inadequate. If she hasn't noticed already, she will when she's expected to pour herself into a hole.

Isolde   In our deli the placenta cakes are positively squirting with grade-A fruit toppings!

Claudia   There are usually good, upstanding people sitting in this room, one good woman next to another. Hold on to the handbag and the small change! Some foreigner has the master key and we're at the keyhole. What does that leave? Desirable women in the midst of the specially designed parts of their bodies! Take another swig!

Isolde   We're doing the choosing today. We selected the bear and the moose in the ad. They are supposed to be tall, in love with life and photogenic into the bargain.

Claudia   Most women are happy to be perceived. Have already chosen. Our husbands only long for what they already have.

Isolde   This moose and this bear lead pretty disorderly lives. They sent this letter to us. Trousers down, fur to one side, and their thingy is already back in the tunnel where it won't be dazzled by the glare of oncoming headlights.

Claudia   They can take us right along with them, us and our beavers, which are wide open and begging for it.

Isolde   Men always have to see images of our machinery before they know what can be done with it.

Claudia   Before they can operate us. They grant us no power over them.

Isolde   If they're alone they pick up the phone, call anyone at all, and their trousers bang painfully into the backs of their knees over and over again.

Claudia   And soon everyone's turning up in droves, happy as pigs in shit.

A siren sounds.

Waiter's voice (*from the tape*)   No. Don't worry! The siren only means that someone is just trying to steal your car. All part of our special range of services.

The two women jump up, knickers still round their ankles, and stumble to the exit, peer out briefly, shrug their shoulders and come back again. They both pull up their trousers and place their bottles on the ledge in front of the mirrors. They begin to touch up their make-up and hair-dos.

Isolde Do you think we should cork up the bottles?

Claudia Better had. Otherwise it'll only get out.

Isolde Smooth as a spirit. Wasn't worth the effort. Can't get another note out of my tired reed into the instrument. Be nice to pump up the volume a bit.

Claudia We're rising up out of our situation for once. We've purchased triumphant shoes.

Isolde Looking stunning for a wild night is a thing of the past. Who sees the smooth skin living after the latest fashion in the grave of my body?

Claudia I just hope we understood the ad right.

Isolde Even if we did, you still have to examine a man very carefully indeed if you want to see whether there's a label sewn into his lining.

Claudia Ours are Moose and Bear Brand. Made like the clothes in Italy, that's what they wrote. We wrote: The more the merrier. Easy come, easy go.

Isolde I feel rather uneasy at the prospect of having to project Kurt's face onto that of a total stranger. Usually I'm glad not to see him at all.

Claudia But we didn't stop reading those ads until we'd decided which petroleum was going to send the stains shooting out of our clothes. As living flames!

Isolde Perhaps we'll end up strewn about on the floor?

Claudia (*peers out*) I'll say one thing though: Never, have so many people paraded past our shithouse door with their flies undone. Loneliness travels with the salesman and gets dumped over the back of a chair in a hotel room. But which one?

Isolde Do you think the moose will be the love of my life?

Claudia Before the breakfast things have been cleared from the table and the tune of Herbert's exhaust-pipe has faded away we'll be serving ourselves up all over again.

Isolde As if we'd just come to the boil! A bear rings the doorbell.

Claudia And we appear, hot off the press, a sensation, at the push of a button!

Isolde But only if the lover-man hasn't been reading the magazines he harmonizes with. The women in there have suddenly stopped bearing any resemblance to me.

Claudia Oh to drain the juice from a moose!

Isolde Or from a bear's bazooka, suck on it until it goes bang and discharges itself. What a lot of work! That's when you begin to realize what kind of stuff a person is really made of.

Claudia Wild and raunchy, like animals! We'll soon know more!

Isolde At long last! In front of me, Kurt plays the shy boy who's been saving himself. But behind his back, greed rules supreme. Then he works his bank account off on me. He's given his assets a good coat of grease and stuck them in an investment fund.

Claudia Good and early in the morning, before I have to leave for the surgery, I am forced by Herbert to return inside my sex because I've forgotten something there: his!

Isolde They know from just one look: we can never leave them. I'll never be enough of a looker to be taken out again.

Claudia We are chained to the household as products.

Isolde For them, that's a good enough reason to hop into the car and carry on on their own. Which peasant woman from the Innviertel would want to possess my Kurt? None! I quite understand them.

Claudia   Which white-collar thirty-something would want to possess my Herbert? Quite a few! For the simple reason that he made no truthful statements about his dimensions in the sauna club.

Isolde   Better to look for new contacts! A hairy bag of fickle tricks opens up. But one false move into the light is enough to ruin the whole film beyond repair. A film they all wanted to see in order to find out what they should be doing with us next.

Waiter's voice (*from the tape*)   Props at the ready! Return to the vicinity! Hygiene!

Claudia   I'm afraid we'll have to carry the can for this outing on our own.

Isolde   The never-changing image they have of themselves and of us on this film can be fatal. Someday I'll find myself standing before my master and he won't recognize his own dog.

Claudia   Look, my costume! The ribbon stretched taut between my thighs. It says: Sex is sport! In the plasticsmith's workshop secrets are forged while we're still hot.

Isolde   Yes. The images of the female sex are more like images of sport. My sport consists of having to take leave of myself incessantly. My furrow presses itself into this snazzy sport ribbon for all to see, that's why the leotard was purchased. Its colour is poison to the eye. Make the seed bear fruit, Mister Moose!

Claudia   Sex is looking and then performing.

Isolde   Sex is looking and then putting one's inner hound-dog through its paces.

Claudia   Herbert's body got up on tiptoes yesterday.

Isolde   Yes, you've already told me. And then he frothed at the gills and spat it out.

Claudia We wanted somebody else to preside over our daily trials and tribulations who could then be condemned to us.

Isolde Footsteps come alongside us, open us up. No one closes the door behind us.

There is a discrete knocking at the door, the women turn towards it. Their husbands come in disguised as **Moose** *and* **Bear**. *The costumes don't fit them, are too large for them. The moose steps on his robe and stumbles. The bear has to gather his robe together at the front. They both talk into contact microphones which make their voices somewhat artificial. Echo! Reverb!*

Herbert May we join you, dear ladies?

Kurt Don't let our immensity alarm you!

Herbert We were made for the night. Illuminated bars, where people pour themselves down each others throats, lull us into our false sense of destiny. Not to mention our dexterity!

Kurt We're so wrapped up in our costumes that we can't see where we're putting our feet.

Herbert We can't spread our wings just at the moment because we have to hold on to our costumes.

Kurt Could you suggest anything? We would gladly donate ourselves! You placed an advert, didn't you Karin, and . . . (*Moves toward* **Claudia** *threateningly.*)

Herbert Emma! What kind of people like watching Formula One racing on TV the most? Those without a driving licence! (*He moves threateningly toward* **Isolde**.) What did you write in the ad?

Kurt That you're inviting us to your own private knees-up?

Herbert That you'll be the very last ones to pass out? All the others have long since passed away.

Kurt But we can't see where they've gone.

Herbert What have we here? Two of a kind seek similar couple who are just the same.

They move towards the women who back off a little.

Isolde Excellent! I'm Emma!

Claudia Most excellent! I'm Karin!

Isolde But you wrote in the ad that you were above average height.

Herbert That's because later on we're going to eat cold chicken and pickled gherkins. Because *our* reserves have been plundered *too*.

Kurt We would be glad to replenish your stockings, ladies! Let's see, what've we got? The choice is ours!

Herbert Wait and see!

Isolde Excellent! You really want *me*? You're not mistaken?

Claudia Mega-excellent!

Isolde Super! But you wrote in the ad that our birthday suits were tailor-made for each other, a perfect fit!

Claudia Fantastic! Just look how well your outfit fits! Suits you down to the ground!

The man dressed as a baby comes crawling in through the door, cries 'Mama, Mama', and clings tightly to **Claudia** *who shakes him off and kicks him down off her. The 'Baby' bawls frightfully.*

Isolde Elephantastic! Here comes the Home Guard!

The baby tries it with her and is given the same treatment.

Isolde The baby ruffian rhyming and climbing. Terrific! After that it'll take nothing short of a professional snooze to put us to sleep.

Kurt Our bodies are one big banquet which we've cooked up. In my defence I must say that I will have rather overexerted myself in bed beforehand.

Isolde   On the one hand I do believe that you're a moose but on the other hand I don't believe it after all. Are you sure you mean me?

During what follows, the baby crawls around and plays the baby. For example, he grabs the bottles and tries to drink out of them. They are taken away from him. Pantomime. He is treated very roughly which only seems to turn him on.

Claudia   On the one hand I do believe that you're a bear but on the other hand I don't believe it after all.

Isolde   How can you feel a sense of inner well-being when you don't even seem to be a match for yourself?

Herbert   Having escorted many vivacious women, I know from experience that even the smallest things can stir them up beyond all measure. We are above average size, however you look at it. And here, if you please!

He opens the door and tries to drag in a huge trunk which he left outside, but it won't fit through and he pushes it back out.

Herbert   Full MOT: the potency machine from Munich! Costs eight marks and fits in any trouser pocket!

Kurt   Ensures durability: an electromagnetic field is generated. Then a kind of bulb comes and breaks the circuit: a mere scratch on the polished piano and hey presto! Most highly favoured Lady!

Herbert   Makes an upright man of you. Ensures growth below the belt.

Claudia   Great!

Isolde   Just great!

Herbert   You girls should see us when we've spent a few hours in your nether orifices! How stupendous we look then!

Claudia   Classic. Multiple orgasm here I come!

Isolde   No sense in the senses. No trains of thought on the tracks where my body runs.

Claudia Great! With a smart man who's somehow not really real.

Isolde You did say earlier on that we'd get slaughtered later at the cold buffet?

Herbert We said, after the shagging comes the slaughter at the cold buffet.

Isolde Simply a cut above the rest!

Kurt But not a word about home! Nothing about what you like doing, sport or art. Ski? Not likely!

Herbert We only make withdrawals on our capital in exceptional cases.

Kurt But we regret it immediately after shooting our wads when the accounts show that we should have minded our own business! Later on we need it, but by then it's dissolved into reality.

Claudia Yes. It comes but once.

Herbert Until now, very few women have rubbed us up the right way. Sad but true.

Claudia Excellent. (*Cheers.*) Yeah! Yeah! Yeah!

Isolde First rate! But your ad told a far less droopy story.

Claudia Your picture spoke more than a thousand words. Were they the wrong ones?

Isolde Bingo! Just great! My picture wasn't me either.

Claudia Your feet, in particular, come to an end much sooner in reality than you claimed in the ad.

Isolde You really are a very unusual specimen, Mister Moose. Excellent!

Claudia The bear seems a bit short on the stuffing too. Simply first rate!

She kicks against the bear's fur and he nearly falls over.

Claudia You're a total knock-over! Excellent!

Herbert   I haven't even got started yet! Original photo, my arse! And where's your original cunt, 'Karin'?

Kurt   I'm well-suited for Algerian, for what it's worth, on account of my size. Which means there's room inside me for more than just food!

Herbert   We are the originals! Anything else you see must be a copy of us.

Claudia   Yes! Smashing! First rate! Hot pants!

Kurt   The unreal lives within what's real. Our furs conceal the not-yet-real.

Herbert   There is a certain full-bodiedness to me which acts as a support for the fur.

Claudia   The way you said that was just splendid!

Herbert   Get your bodies to safety!

Kurt   We will now make an effort to come, but it will be a moment before our rise and fall. Please wait, 'Emma'! Please wait! Please wait! (*Like a recorded message.*)

Claudia   Grrrrrrreat!

Isolde   Colossal! Simply intramuscular!

All four scream demonstratively.

Herbert   We don't want to know what you do for a living because we'll soon be going our separate ways again.

Kurt   It doesn't matter, 'Emma'.

Claudia   Cool!

Herbert   For modern Greek games and affectionate jiggery-pokery it doesn't matter whether you're raking in the fallen leaves in your garden or whether there's been yet another drop in numbers.

Claudia   I'm flabbergasted.

Isolde   I'm totally beside myself. Not me any more.

The fake bear and the fake moose now begin to paw the women and to drag them into separate cubicles. The women giggle and squeal.

Isolde Stop! The written details have to be checked first! To see whether what you wrote tallies with what you're doing!

Claudia In the midst of your sawdust you don't look like you could bend even a single straw with all your huffing and puffing!

Kurt I'm supposed to have written that? Something that would never even have crossed my mind? You whore! You're ripping my fondest memories out of me!

Isolde You look like an earplug in a lughole.

Herbert I come from afar, a dream come true. And you'll be able to say you were there when it happened, 'Karin'!

Kurt How can air be so heavy?

Both women scream in unison as if they were on a spit. This should be comical rather than frightening. Like a kind of demonstrative cry of woe.

In the cubicles a kind of orgy with giggles and thrashing about, only the occasional foot (paw) can be seen appearing and quickly disappearing again under the doors. Various people make brief entries, some in full costume, some in half costume, some totally without costume. They take photos or short video shots of what's happening in the cubicles.

Herbert (*half suffocating*) First this awkward position and then the struggle to keep it up.

Isolde (*likewise, and thereafter the others too*) You look like something on paper and then all that's revealed is the same old sausage. When *I* put my foot down, on the other hand, the floor's the limit!

Claudia I don't throw anything away unread.

Isolde We'll mop up every last blob of mustard you throw into our laps.

Claudia   How about performing that bodily gesture a little less aimlessly?

Herbert   Ouch! I don't know where this heaviness of mine is coming from. So sorry!

Kurt   My fur coat protects me from becoming too well acquainted with a person, thank God.

Claudia   Help! Help me! A bear!

Isolde   Help! Please help! A live moose!

Both scream in unison, as above.

Herbert   I lay claim to life! Breathe warmth into cupped paws.

Isolde   Breathe into the cups we've washed up. To see if there's any of us left stuck to them. Help! To the rescue!

Claudia   You'd love that wouldn't you. To ruffle us up with your hurly-burly. Help!

Herbert   In a second you'll feel like you're being hosed down with a jet of water!

Isolde   Go on then, give me the object in question! Let's see what appears! I'm out of it.

Claudia   So do you *always* live in this little room and play the animal? Or just in summer?

Isolde   What *are* you doing down there? One brief glance outside your fur coat should tell you where a culture has been bred in a dish.

Claudia   And anyway – any hospital has more breeding in it than you.

Isolde   Bloody marvellous! Help! HELP! A moose that's still alive!

Claudia   Splendid! To the rescue! A lively bear! Such a heavy animal!

Isolde   Just you let a moose sit on you sometime!

Claudia   Just you let a bear sit on your lap sometime!

Isolde   This animal fur is just decoration for something that lives inside them, or at least in their suits, and which has been donated to us. I wonder if I can keep it down?

Claudia   We can't wait around for hours for an animal to come along with his bleeding soul in his mouth, only to find that it doesn't even belong to him. The animal removed it from somewhere else.

Isolde   And we're supposed to do a sewing job on his fur coat.

Claudia   Ouch! Help! A living bear! We'd agreed on that, but not that he'd then behave like a human!

Isolde   To the rescue! A lively moose! We were expecting that, but we weren't expecting one to actually come.

Claudia   We don't need that kind of costume. We're more than just a pair of pretty Polaroids!

They both scream again, but comically, not with terror or anxiety.

Herbert   Please now slip your contribution to our expenses under the pocket of the costume!

Kurt   Now that we've broken a taboo, please stick the service charge under the zip of the costume, here!

The thrashing about behind the doors dies down, a few stragglers take photos, then gradually calm.

Kurt (*breathing heavily, like the others after him, slowly but calming*)   I don't know how to do this costume up again.

Herbert   We borrowed it and now it's become heavily attached to us.

Kurt   Befitting our own heavyweight status, which includes a measure of hot air.

Claudia   You weren't very skilled at nurturing a woman, age and status unimportant, into full bloom.

Isolde   You, Mister Moose, remind me of the male half of a couple who doesn't like looking for something in vain. I then have to go and fetch it for him.

Kurt   You halogenetic bitch!

Claudia   Did you know, my partner's only source of pleasure is seeing me in the wrong. His views, you see, would all fit on a single picture postcard.

Herbert   You fucking bitch!

Claudia   Now you've brought out parts of your body which get bored in their clothing like people in a rainy park or a museum.

Isolde   We couldn't have predicted someone like you. We simply haven't begun to get worked up into a frenzy. Doesn't matter!

Kurt   Dirty bitch!

Claudia   Someone like you has to add something extra to the beast inside so that one notices you've been here at all.

Herbert   Fucking bitch! Slut!

Isolde   When a doggy goes walkies it should know the route to escape by in case a stronger animal turns up.

Herbert   What a bitch! She's talking about us too!

Kurt   You just want to cash in on the aura which radiates from our economic power! Sluts! Sluts the lot of you! 'Karin' and 'Emma'!

Claudia   We're not rising to this glockenspiel. Kindly give us some peace! Put a sock in it!

Isolde   They sound like our husbands would if we cut the thread of their life by cutting off the television.

Claudia   But there's no juice shooting down the chicken wire into the battery where all their eggs are laid in one basket.

Kurt   Bitches! Bitches! Bitches!

Herbert   Get out of my life! You've covered me in your mucus! My lovely costume! Dirty bitch!

Claudia   We can't believe what we're seeing. Just animals!

Kurt We have to take off the animal now because you've made us dirty!

Isolde And you've peed on me. Can't you be more careful! The good Lord left a hole in animals too! They just have to know where it is!

Kurt I've always wanted to. But my wife won't stand for anything of the sort. She'd be straight on the phone to the Furniture Rescue Squad.

Herbert Would you mind washing out my costume for me? It's only borrowed.

Kurt That's what comes of Nature blazing a trail for itself. It's not altogether not their fault!

Claudia Animals are never modest. Constantly munching their way through the forest.

Herbert Bigger animals are always looming over our bushels and pissing on our fireworks.

Kurt Just because I dress up as a bigger animal doesn't mean that I am one.

Claudia Why don't you take off the bear's head, you'll suffocate if you don't raise your oxygen levels! We don't want your other attempts to be failures too!

Isolde Please understand, your oxygen levels aren't the only things that need raising! You see! Like this! Oh, it doesn't work! It just doesn't work.

Claudia This one doesn't work either. Help! An animal! A great big animal!

Isolde To the rescue! It's an animal! A real, solid animal in a furry cover!

Claudia Yes, an undercover animal.

Herbert When women get physical! There's just no stopping them.

Kurt As far as lighting their fire is concerned, I seem to have run out of steam.

Herbert It's time we introduced ourselves, you bastard. But for the moment I can't get my face off.

Kurt Me neither. Mine's sitting squarely on my contentment and expressing itself!

Claudia An animal! Help! Help!

Isolde A real animal! To the rescue!

Claudia You pricks! Your faces won't be any better! How peculiar! An animal!

Herbert If you would only help me reveal myself in a serious light.

Kurt If you could only lose just once you'd already have won me over.

Herbert Don't start listing all the other things you'd like. Because I can't do it again. Not satisfied?

Claudia Is there not going to be anyone who can do it better?

Isolde An animal on the loo. That's quite something, even if it didn't perform very well.

Claudia An animal on the loo, that's unusual. Even if it didn't find the hole.

Isolde An animal that pees next to the hole can't know many other tricks.

Claudia The question is, do we consider them capable of eating anything that isn't waiting obediently for them in a bowl?

Isolde Even though animals have heads *and* tails, it's always got to be a toss up. They'll never learn. Good-naturedness soon gets on one's nerves. And wildness isn't everyone's cup of tea either.

Claudia They're sure to have their good sides, like anyone else.

Isolde Madness! Animals on the toilet!

Claudia   Craziness! Animals on the loo!

Herbert   What it said in the ad wasn't true.

Kurt   It simply isn't true that one person can provide treatment of any kind all on his own. You need the right equipment. And we need to be so inclined before we can start going downhill.

Claudia   How a person looks is never true either.

Isolde   Ever heard of an animal assessing itself realistically in the mirror?

Claudia   I brake gladly if I see a deer on the road.

Isolde   The moose will brake of his own accord when he sees our sexy underwear.

Claudia   When an animal in human clothing resembles a human in human clothing, then one is powerless.

Isolde   The body is just the bodywork. People are rocked back and forth inside it until they finally quieten down.

Waiter's voice (*from the tape*)   Now make your way to our car park! Wear something funny! Pretend to attend! Some persons will be of no use. But we even have an alternative programme from which mature, chubby women can distance themselves. You too will have a tuning fork stuck into your flesh and strike a popular note. Examine yourselves with a critical eye! Others will be much more critical!

The ladies rush out, half-dressed, followed by the men, who get tangled up in each other since they have now completely lost control over their costumes.

Act Three

*The car park, in the foreground a car. There must be the usual
atmosphere of a car park at night – most importantly the headlights
flashing past, the cars hissing by, the rumbling etc. Shrubbery, the rise
of an embankment. Overflowing rubbish bins. People flit past through
the night, in various states of dress and undress. Middle-aged
housewives in sexy underwear – please consult contact magazines for
inspiration! One is disguised as a white bunny. The imagination is set
no limits that wouldn't be set in home videos. Please make everything
cheap and shabby: concrete toilet block, etc. etc. The two women
Claudia and **Isolde** as 'Karin' and 'Emma', come in, moving like
speed skaters, as a pair next to each other, this has to be choreographed.
They'll just have to practise! Behind them the two men **Herbert** and
Kurt with the same movements. They are still wearing their costumes
but they have taken them half off like overalls, i.e. they're letting the
upper part hang down. They have trouble with the ice skating. The
speed skating may be interrupted from time to time for a bit of paired
figure-skating, each man briefly lifts up one of the women, they may even
fling them away a little, that all depends on the physical suppleness of
the actresses and actors. After a while the men sit down.*

*On the embankment, which is thinly covered with grass mixed with
litter, as one would expect, the two genuine animals, **Bear** and
Moose. The **Bear** is sitting on its hind paws, totally animal-like
Being, and eating away at a nice little cadaver, the identity of which
(animal or human) is not clearly visible. The **Moose** has its front
legs propped on the embankment and is grazing on grass, herbs and
shrubs. The two animals' shadows make them seem to take on
disturbing, gigantic proportions.*

*During the following dialogues: At irregular intervals, men and
women with or without costume, also in various states of dress and
undress, should jump on the speakers, pull them to the ground or get
stuck into them in some other way, and allow themselves to be almost
pulled along, until they are shaken off by the person speaking. Please*

draw inspiration from commercial porno films! Throughout the whole play a cheap, rather miserable effect should be created, as already mentioned. A good start is only half the battle, after all!

Isolde   Even taking into account the fact that they were well out of their depth in those furs, that was one big disappointment.

Claudia   Even fish make nicer playmates than them. My husband wants to read about fishing and get his tackle out on the riverbank. But that animal didn't even think about what it wanted. I should have recommended a good tailor for some alterations to its fur coat, then it might have fitted in with us a bit better.

Isolde   Kurt is very much his own zone, a territory hemmed in on all sides by outlandish garments. But your bear could have done a few turns in his robe if he'd only wanted to.

Claudia   I get the impression there was something pushing the moose's body out at the forehead. There's no point placing ads just to not get something one's never had anyway.

Isolde   A murderer would be a fine figure of hope for a woman. His behaviour gets more and more interesting as long as the papers don't lose interest. He puts himself on show in a leather coat, the coat contains a dangerous portent.

Claudia   If you're going to choose a costume like that then you should at least be able to fill it out.

Isolde   And get your body back in working order if it changes for the worse for any reason.

Claudia   At least Herbert is occasionally tidy before he messes me up again.

Isolde   'Karin', who the hell sent us off along life's great highway just to plague us with an endless succession of roadworks?

Claudia   Just to leave us standing there. You find yourself sitting in the same boat as someone who thinks he's the boat itself and who won't stop looking for holes.

Isolde   Disappointing experience.

She kicks the **Moose** *in the side in passing. The animal sways a little, but then goes on grazing.*

Claudia   Hey you! Did it say sperm-thirsty babe or sperm-thirsty bitch in the ad? Animals are to keep quiet in the forest, that's the rule for all woodland ramblers. I lay myself out ready on the new cover our couch got for Christmas. Our flat is cleaned so that Herbert can use it as a swamp to wade through once a week. Stands himself up next to the flowers. People as full as department stores wait irritably for their chance to sink their arms into other people up to the hilt. Success? Arms chewed off down to the bone! As if I were a pile of reduced items!

Isolde (*gives the* **Bear** *a wide berth, the* **Bear** *amiably offers her a piece of meat*)   I stretch my body out like a cushion. Although I'm not drugged, I am attacked in my sleep by someone who has my own tights wrapped crookedly around his hands. Women! We are conspicuous even if we just get undressed. We look different from them. How very unwise of us!

Claudia (*she prods the* **Bear** *absent-mindedly with a stick. It doesn't react. To the* **Bear**)   You didn't have the guts to murder us, huh? Guess we weren't your type, eh? Your type are nice young girls from whom you can take a piece of flesh as a souvenir to be placed like a wax effigy in front of an offertory box, with a prayer to the Saint: Please give me a raging hard-on like that again sometime.

Isolde   I am an older woman. I am the nothing from which nothing comes. I will soon return to dust. There we were, looking for attention, but really we were past it far too quickly.

Claudia   Let's carry on dribbling our ball so that we can make a pass to someone else who's learnt how to shoot. So that we soar up, up and away from ourselves at last.

Absent-mindedly pats the hind quarters of the **Moose** *which looks round briefly and then continues to graze.*

Claudia (*to the* **Moose**)   Have you ever already stormed your prey before noticing that you're only a herbivore?

Moose   Often!

Claudia   The way my husband Herbert does it, socks fly into the corner and truncheons fly from the hip. He himself gets stuck in the mud in front of the television.

Isolde   In situations like that, Kurt carefully lets the motor roll back into his vehicle. Just so that he can be some kind of driving force again.

Claudia (*offers the* **Moose** *a scrunched-up food wrapper to eat. The* **Moose** *smells it, shakes its head decisively, takes another thorough sniff and then carries on grazing*)   One arranges for oneself to appear in a proper advert so that one is in the newspaper in extended form. And then one is simply declared unfit for service.

Isolde (*to the* **Moose**)   Mister Animal, why didn't you stand as tall as you said in your description?

Claudia (*to the* **Bear**)   Why, Mister Predator, didn't you stand tall at all? And why did you claim afterwards that we'd had a terrific orgasm? Only we didn't notice it.

Isolde   We are working animals, unlike you! (*Smacks the* **Moose** *on the rump, harder than the last time, the animal walks a few steps and then continues grazing.*)

The men have sat themselves down. A procession à la A Midsummer Night's Dream *quickly crosses the stage, unprofessional and disorganized, like a playgroup putting on a show in pathetic, home-made costumes. Flower and animal costumes, but pathetic and ill-fitting. Including some children!*

Kurt (*making a grab at the procession*)   Come over here and get some sweeties! Are you a ghostly apparition? All grey and hopping around in a net?

Herbert (*likewise*) Have you been translated? That's good. We want to use the infant sex for our own ends too so that our fun is redoubled!

Kurt Are you really truly beautiful? Not just when your mothers in their fleshpots see you fly past at ultrasonic velocity?

Man in disguise They hang around in the nest. Dangerous portents!

Woman in disguise I'll walk up and down so you see I'm not afraid!

Child We're running, master, we're running!

Child Don't follow me and don't lead me about a round! Through bog, through bush, through brake, through briar!

Child Appear not as werewolf nor as fire. I'm not mad but I'm beginning to burn because of you!

Child Don't want to neigh, bark, grunt or roar. I don't imitate voices! Where that's concerned I'm all my own work.

Child Not flames! Not like horse, hound, hog, bear, fire at every turn!

Man in disguise Must I speak now? No. I'm just going off to remove the source of a noise. I'll be right back.

Man in disguise If I had wit enough to get out of this wood then I'd have just as much as I needed.

Child (*struggles against **Herbert** who tries to grab it*) Take care that you don't get swallowed up by a beef roast!

Herbert (*tries to pull the **Child** towards him, but it manages to tear itself free and run away with the other members of the procession*) Hello, child! You beast of burden! You simply have to bear my brunt!

Kurt Isolde just begrudges this child my great body!

Herbert Because the child has smoother skin and always wants to run away wherever its ball takes it. In the end, a woman is all one has left. That's what it's like with Claudia:

she has no way of knowing who the man was who spread himself out beneath her.

Exit the procession.

Kurt   They've gone. Isolde is accustomed to me and me alone. That's why there's no way I could ever have appealed to her in a costume.

Herbert   If only I'd remained myself! As the property owner said to the lay of the land.

Kurt   We could have had anything from them if they'd only still been children!

Herbert   Why on earth did they suddenly insist on half an hour's foreplay? That's far more than what they really need.

Kurt   One wishes to stick one's cock in their cunts, for a moment at least, to clean it before the big squirt, and they go and pull it out by the short and curlies.

Herbert   That's enough to give anyone cold feet.

Kurt   One of the two animal gentlemen must have offered to give Isolde some accompaniment on her solo number beforehand. Rabble! Pack!

Herbert   The start of a fraudulent marathon. But much more sinister. Not like us.

Kurt   Those two animals? But that's not allowed!

Herbert   Beseige tour buses. Beg for food. Won't refuse anything. Dark and hairy.

Kurt   A veritable infestation!

Herbert   Like animals. Horny without a cause. The Doesn't-Matter-Horn.

Kurt   Has-beens, sent to stand outside the gates of hell because they wanted to smoke one last cigarette. Hesitantly. The scrunched-up newspaper with the job offers clenched like a gent's handbag in their fists. That bag can contain a lethal weapon, at any moment.

Herbert   Still stiff from the sperm that's come their way.

Kurt Closely examining the furniture and household textiles they found beside our wives. Railcar drivers who've only just come racing out of the tunnel of their instincts and already blown a gasket.

Herbert They must have answered an ad! Only thing that makes sense.

Kurt Our wives have been looking around with more interest than we'd have thought them capable of. Minutes later a huge animal appears out of the forest, buckling at the knees.

Herbert And we thought that after all these years we'd wiped that contented look off their faces with our powerful fingers.

Kurt Out of the water closet, anal fans! And onto the football pitch! The arses move faster out there!

Waiter's voice (*from the tape*) You are now tearing apart all nets and edifices in which you've come across creepy crawlies. Meanwhile, we've been putting together a video which will make short work of you! To be precise, the film will be shown on the screen we've set up for you in that spanking new, cherry-red Audi 80 over there on the right! Long live the forest! Gather round, the images are still warm! This fodder is about to be served up, please step forward! If your backside needs a lesson or two, then get stuck in, you scallywags! This is your club! You're all in it together! It's the place to be!

In the aforementioned car – no matter what make, depends on the sponsor, could be a BMW or whatever – a glowing screen appears in front of the driver's seat. The interior of the car is filled with a ghostly light like a tabernacle shrine. Those present form a tight knot in front of the glowing vehicle in their costumes. They look through the windows and doors at the video screen in the interior. Our foursome join in. Only the animals pause briefly but then continue to graze.

Isolde (*to* **Claudia** *as they stroll over. Their husbands were quicker and are already pushing their way to the front in amongst the other participants.*) That's us!

Claudia   It must be us! Light streaming to its us-shaped convergence! We're on television!

Isolde   But it's only a private channel.

Claudia   I looked into the wide-open mouth of an animal about to scream and I'd like to see that again now.

Isolde   They just open their beaks like ours at home. All our gracefulness was in vain.

Claudia   Sons in the prime of life are smashed to pieces by war but we're not even permitted to snap up ten decagrammes of dangerous living.

Isolde   My neck has been known to crunch between Kurt's teeth. Who'll swap me ten good years, the last ten that is, for a newer, fuller figure? The cake which life has pressed out of me is now rolling towards me like an avalanche. Fresh young things are waiting for Kurt in the bushes, and they don't like to be kept waiting.

Claudia   This bear quite seriously referred to his achievement as a yearning.

Isolde   Anything's more exciting than Kurt when he sinks back into his seat. He's already lost all his fluids doing 180 in the fast lane.

Claudia   We should have put plastic covers on the seats.

Isolde   They don't even let their inner hound-dog run wild. Whistle it back pronto. And it comes running, tame like us.

From the car, flickering lights and groans of pleasure. The audience crowds around.

Claudia   Come on, quick! Or we'll not see anything.

Isolde   Those two imitation leopard skins finished quicker than they wanted to.

Claudia   Were we too modest? If we placed an ad the only answers would be sure to come from elderly gents who don't have any daytime fun in their day centres.

Isolde   Old-age bachelors whose contacts with their toe-nails have all been severed by life. False teeth swimming next to them in a glass. Their denture fluid is more active than they are. I'll soon be the same. I'm all shipshape now and my Bristols are still in fashion but I'll soon be a complete wreck.

They both look into the car. Enthusiasm.

Claudia   That's us! Great!

Isolde   Yeah, that's us! Funtastic! Look, 'Karin'! Look, the outline of an animal head from behind, and there, a mouth, maybe mine, hung between its hind paws like a teabag. Lovely!

Claudia   Herbal tea, if that. Funtabulous. A position which life had always denied us up to now. We look good, I find. So homely, because we've known each other such a long time. Great!

Isolde   And now – Never tasted so good! – Now he's getting out his pecker for a wank but then reconsiders and holds it out to you. Or is that me? Smart! Crazy, really crazy! But I know that size. Where have I seen it before?

Claudia   I know that format from somewhere too. Not bad. But next time it'll be us calling the shots. We don't want anyone getting in there before us again!

Isolde   But we'll have to be careful, otherwise the men will believe there are as many possibilities as we make out, and then they won't contact us.

Claudia   I've seen these features many times before, but in a different setting. Well-hung but always hanging.

Isolde   This figure is a regular guest of mine, maybe it even lives with me!

Claudia   As if the entire population of Leoben were standing behind us with brochures.

Isolde   Herbert! My God! Herbert! Then that must be Kurt! It's true he doesn't much like getting up. Kurt! You were great! Brilliant! (*Pushes her way through to* **Kurt**.)

Claudia   If that's Kurt then that must be Herbert. You
were terrific, Herbert, you were never that good before you
put on a costume! Resurrected from apparent death!
Unique! Naughty! Just get a load of this person's essence!
Isn't it just international?!

Isolde   Just get a load of Kurt! How he's waxing, I mean
wanking. Say something! Show us your wotsit! Yes! That's
the way!

Claudia   Just imagine, on holiday by Lake Balaton, six
more people could join in, absolute humans with souls to
match! Superb. Patent Hungarian couples! Excellent! And
none of them can believe their eyes, so their fingers have to
give them a helping hand or two! (*Very loud groaning from the
tape.*)

Isolde   In this shot I'm looking calmly at my partner. No
danger of my understanding him.

Claudia   Extraterrestrial, Herbert! How you find the
image of Woman and then colour it in all on your own!

Isolde   If Mother Nature hadn't wanted you that way,
Kurt, she would never have given you such prominent
contours.

Claudia   It was simply ... simply ... of course, it was
simple!

Isolde   Kurt, it was as if your vital statistics and your
ecstatic vitality had been fastened to you on a scrap of paper.
That was the price.

Claudia   Not all women are as radiant and pneumatic as
us, you know.

Isolde   Not *pneumatic*, Claudia, come on! *Automatic*, with
radials!!

Claudia   Holidays by motorail. That's why you were so
good, Herbert. Poetry in motion, because you were so
relaxed on arrival.

Isolde   Super! Counter-megalithic! Extra-ragadocious!

The women literally jump on their husbands, hang on them, the men, somewhat indignant and offended, shake them off. A brief bout of wrestling which is watched with interest by the spectators.

Isolde   Now listen to me, Kurt.

Claudia   Now mark my words to the letter, Herbert!

Herbert   A man thinks he's returning to hearth and home, only to be greeted by the imminent arrival of twosomes who've been spelled out in block capitals under WANTED. Along with their knobs and knockers. By a policeman. In the cellblock of life.

Kurt   Sex rides with a person's entire body and soul loaded onto the pillion seat behind it – as merchandise. These one-track vehicles! Danger! Danger! Humans are perpetually using their own sex to brake with!

Herbert   The wandering is at an end when you begin to feel at home. You do not become one of the natives just because you're too tired to wander.

Kurt   You girls have obviously forgotten your destinations.

Claudia   It was you and you alone that we saw fighting valiantly in the cavernous depths of the animals.

Isolde   It was clear to us from the start that the men inside the beasts could only have been you.

Claudia   We run all this way for an animal and in the end it's always just you.

They drape themselves around the men and are dragged along a little way. The men hurry, wheezing and furious, towards the two totemic animals who stop eating and become attentive. Before they've even got their breath back, the men start hitting the animals.

Bear (*shrinks from the blows and holds out a piece of meat as if making a peace offering*)   Here! A chunk for you? Enough here for everyone.

Moose (*likewise*)   Peace, I beseech you! (*Moves slightly to one side. Gets hit.*) Enough grass here to feed everyone. I'll gladly

budge up a bit. We all have our place on earth and the
heavens act in mysterious ways from above.

Bear   What my colleague says is true. Where eating is
concerned we animals are inseparable, because one eats the
other.

Moose   I stick to a herbal diet myself. I can't compete with
you!

Kurt (*kicks the* **Moose** *so hard in the side that it nearly
falls*)   Stop, foreigner! Always have to mess up what is holy
to us.

Herbert   Useless beings! No animal has ever been seen to
draw back from a table when invited.

Kurt   These creatures with their plastic forms (*Kicks.*)
want either to get to know us or to eat us out of house and
home.

Herbert   Take our women away from us.

Kurt   They're only women because we're men. Then
comes the night. A stranger disguised as sex forces his way in
between us and God.

Herbert   Get out of here! Get out of here!

Bear   Please help us eat! It's a free-for-all! (*Sways.*)

Moose   Enough room for everyone. (*Sways.*)

Herbert   All you do is hang around like private parts
making work for us! Get out!

Kurt   You just remind us of the darkness within ourselves!
Out! Out! Out!

*Now the other participants in the orgy begin to crowd towards the
animals and to shower them with blows.*

Isolde   Poor little creatures! They've never hurt anybody!
(*Hits.*)

Claudia   The very essence of sobriety! The opposite of
humans. They're definitively innocent! (*Hits.*)

Isolde   Your little joyride is over, because you have no master. No more foraging and snuffling and pissing all over the place! You can't just go gadding about and ignore appearances! (*Hits.*) Such poor animals! So innocent.

Claudia   Nature is always the answer to stupid questions. (*Hits.*) No more running through the night for you! Get dark yourself! Be more like us! Be more like us!

The animals disappear in the mass of people.

Kurt   Race off across the plains. You can't stay here.

Herbert   You're like nuisances at a nudist beach. We want to be the only wild things around here!

Bear   Ow! You've forgotten our minds. (*Collapses.*)

Moose   Ooch! Ouch! I wanted nothing but the very best for you. Has anyone noticed how gentle I am? (*Collapses.*)

Both animals are literally buried by the humans.

Bear (*expires*)   You can have my food now.

Moose (*likewise*)   You can have my patch of earth now.

Kurt   Away with them! The pot already has us cooking in it!

Herbert   Precisely. We are our own staple diet.

*The group now gathers round on the ground. They have eaten pieces of meat from the animals and are beginning to gnaw on the bones. Suddenly, out of the empty animal furs that are spread out on the ground crawl two Japanese philosophy students, clearly visible, dressed in smart suits and wearing ties, it is totally obvious that it was them inside the animals all the time. They are carrying Sony Electronic Books — promotion effect! — from which they read their lines. They climb untouched out of the furs, move away from the group of people eating and walk downstage. The light from the electronic books casts a bluish glow on their faces. I call them **S1** and **S2**.*

*Upstage, the feasting orgy, throwing bones over their shoulders.
Screens are now showing nice animal films in which bears and moose
stand around intact and happy, eating or being eaten. The students
speak with great calm.*

S1 In the wild there is no thought, just action. Dowsing-
rods held out before us in trembling hands, we are challenged
to read something into this vacuous expanse of evidence and
witness.

S2 Yes. Something which was hidden. Or did we create it
ourselves? Did a human insect crawl out of this form, leaving
its shell behind, or do humans still have to squeeze into the
mould which is there waiting for them?

S1 Cracks open up, signalling the return of the
inexplicable. And then more strange residues which have
retained the form of something, but of what?

S2 We force ourselves upon Nature until all that's left is our
stench and our skeletons.

S1 Why does this space, which was so beautiful, now have
to hold open its own stage curtain and reveal us as products?

S2 Because we want to be bigger than we've ever been,
whereas we can only be as big as the form that was intended
for us.

S1 Should we save ourselves from extinction or not?

S2 Just so that this huge space still has something to offer in
the mail-order catalogue which only ever offers us ourselves,
exclusively. However many instalments we pay, we never
gain full ownership.

S1 We never quite get ourselves together.

S2 But we do leave traces.

S1 Maybe that hidden something has already happened.

S2 What happens is anything but hidden. We're just too
busy looking on the ground for salvageable parts of
ourselves.

S1   How presumptuous we were in trying to produce something to suit us!

S2   Electronics is a veritable miracle! A recording system exists which immediately resolves its subject to the highest dissolution.

S1   It suffices that we are comrades with a common camcorder.

S2   Look! The mountains here are standing together and doing nothing at all, whatsoever.

S1   As long as a trail is laid, no one can deny having been there.

S2   As we are hunted and chased into the woods, we come back as the long-lost echo of a remembered scream.

S1   They've already harvested up anything that was real here into tidy piles.

S2   Which the hunters are grabbing after.

S1   They have a right to their loot, that soft, no-name commodity.

S2   Empty cocoons which these gluttons have long since gnawed their way out of.

S1   They are founded on nothing but themselves.

S2   Judging by appearances, they could well be the start of something terrible.

S1   It would just be them and their evil ways all over again.

S2   Maybe vessels which retain their form long after they have given them the slip.

S1   If and when they turn themselves in it will be too late to reconsider their manufacture.

S2   They'll be there, putting an end to all things they are not.

Curtain

Methuen Modern Plays

include work by

Jean Anouilh
John Arden
Margaretta D'Arcy
Peter Barnes
Sebastian Barry
Brendan Behan
Edward Bond
Bertolt Brecht
Howard Brenton
Simon Burke
Jim Cartwright
Caryl Churchill
Noël Coward
Sarah Daniels
Nick Dear
Shelagh Delaney
David Edgar
Dario Fo
Michael Frayn
John Godber
Paul Godfrey
John Guare
Peter Handke
Jonathan Harvey
Iain Heggie
Declan Hughes
Terry Johnson
Barrie Keeffe
Stephen Lowe

Doug Lucie
John McGrath
David Mamet
Patrick Marber
Arthur Miller
Mtwa, Ngema & Simon
Tom Murphy
Phyllis Nagy
Peter Nichols
Joseph O'Connor
Joe Orton
Louise Page
Luigi Pirandello
Stephen Poliakoff
Franca Rame
Philip Ridley
David Rudkin
Willy Russell
Jean-Paul Sartre
Sam Shepard
Wole Soyinka
C. P. Taylor
Theatre de Complicite
Theatre Workshop
Sue Townsend
Judy Upton
Timberlake Wertenbaker
Victoria Wood

New titles also available from Methuen

John Godber
Lucky Sods & Passion Killers
0 413 70170 0

Paul Godfrey
A Bucket of Eels & The Modern Husband
0 413 68830 5

Jonathan Harvey
Boom Bang-A-Bang & Rupert Street Lonely Hearts Club
0 413 70450 5

Judy Upton
Bruises & The Shorewatchers' House
0 413 70430 0

Phyllis Nagy
Weldon Rising & Disappeared
0 413 70150 6